Library Services to Homeschoolers

Library Services to Homeschoolers

A Guide

Christina Giovannelli-Caputo

ROWMAN & LITTLEFIELD
Lanham • Boulder • New York • London

Published by Rowman & Littlefield
An imprint of The Rowman & Littlefield Publishing Group, Inc.
4501 Forbes Boulevard, Suite 200, Lanham, Maryland 20706
www.rowman.com

6 Tinworth Street, London SE11 5AL, United Kingdom

Copyright © 2022 by The Rowman & Littlefield Publishing Group, Inc.

All rights reserved. No part of this book may be reproduced in any form or by any electronic or mechanical means, including information storage and retrieval systems, without written permission from the publisher, except by a reviewer who may quote passages in a review.

British Library Cataloguing in Publication Information Available

Library of Congress Cataloging-in-Publication Data
Library of Congress Control Number: 2021946772

ISBN 978-1-5381-4681-1 (cloth)
ISBN 978-1-5381-4682-8 (pbk)
ISBN 978-1-5381-4683-5 (electronic)

Contents

	List of Figures	vii
	Foreword	
	Kathy Wentz	ix
	Preface	xiii
	Acknowledgments	xvii
	Introduction	1
Chapter 1	History of Homeschooling	5
Chapter 2	Homeschool Revolution	17
Chapter 3	Homeschooling Today	29
Chapter 4	Different Homeschooling Methods	49
Chapter 5	The Public Library and Homeschoolers	63
Chapter 6	Homeschool Programs and Outreach	77
Chapter 7	Growing Diversity in Home Education	95
Chapter 8	The Future	107
	Index	119
	About the Author	123

List of Figures

Figure 1.1	"Sequoyah, Cherokee Inventor C.B. *King, ca. 1836.*" Library of Congress, LC-DIG-pga-07569.	8
Figure 1.2	Boston Public Latin School Plaque, Boston, Massachusetts. *Daderot.*	9
Figure 1.3	The Dame School. *David Wilkie.*	11
Figure 1.4	Horace Mann, 1850. *Southworth and Hawes.*	12
Figure 2.1	Overcrowded Black School, 1917. *Lewis W. Hine. Library of Congress.*	18
Figure 2.2	John Taylor Gatto. *Thekirbster.*	24
Figure 2.3	What Is Pedagogy? G. *Stanley Hall, 1905.*	25
Figure 3.1	Saint John Catholic School Logan, Ohio, sign states, "Ohio Mandated Closures." *Dan Keck.*	30
Figure 3.2	Day 41 remote school class meeting. *Mario A. Pena.*	31
Figure 3.3	A student learning at home due to COVID-19 school closures. *Christina Giovannelli-Caputo.*	33
Figure 3.4	March 2020 Children and youth out of school due to COVID-19 closures. *Photo Credit: by UN Women.*	36

Figure 3.5	U.S. Department of Agriculture (USDA) Food and Nutrition Service (FNS) National School Lunch Program (NSLP) Seamless Summer Option (SSO) alternative to traditional congregant feeding; this affords safe distancing with curbside distribution during the COVID-19 pandemic in the neighborhoods supported by the Harlandale Independent School District (HISD), in San Antonio, Texas. *USDA*.	38
Figures 4.1–4.3	Three Caputo kids homeschooling during COVID-19. *Christina Giovannelli-Caputo*.	51–52
Figure 4.4	Time4Learning Chart. The following chart from Time4Learning shares differences between classroom instruction and learning in a homeschool setting. *Time4Learning*.	54
Figure 4.5	Recommended Reading on Homeschooling. *Christina Giovannelli-Caputo*.	61
Figure 5.1	Mount Prospect Public Library Homeschooling Brochure. *MPPL*.	68
Figure 5.2	Teacher Library Collaborations Form Christina Giovannelli-Caputo developed to use in a school library system. *Christina Giovannelli-Caputo*.	71
Figure 5.3	Pikes Peak Public Library District Homeschool Take and Make Flyer. *Pikes Peak Public Library District*.	75
Figures 6.1–6.2	Teens learn how to use studio equipment during Homeschool Jam Session Program. *Christina Giovannelli-Caputo*.	83–84
Figure 6.3	Homeschooled youth at homeschool hangout. *Christina Giovannelli-Caputo*.	85
Figures 6.4–6.6	Johnsburg Public Library Homeschool Resource Center. *Christina Giovannelli-Caputo*.	89–90
Figure 7.1	US Census Bureau Household Pulse Survey Weeks 1 and 16, Homeschooling Demographics during COVID-19. *US Census Bureau*.	96
Figures 8.1–8.2	Youth learning from home due to COVID-19, March 2021. *Christina Giovannelli-Caputo*.	112–113
Figure 8.3	Homeschooling child, Fall 2021. *Christina Giovannelli-Caputo*	115

Foreword

Today's homeschool families stand on the shoulders of millions. For thousands of years, parents have taught their children at home. Just as today, parents long ago used their entire world as a curriculum. They found the best resources they could, and parents worked hard to teach their children the skills they would need to know as adults.

As most parents worked the land, preserved their food, made their furniture and clothing, and worked at businesses on their land, their children watched. Children learned their parents' crafts and trades by participating in them. They spent time doing sums for the household. In the quiet of the evenings, they read by firelight. They learned how to work and care for a family and live a balanced life through daily example.

Some larger family compounds could pool together resources and lend a precious book from house to house or share the talents and skills of one adult. If a family had enough money, they could also apprentice their young teens to another family to learn a trade different from theirs.

As early as the 2050s BCE in Egypt, communities developed schools for their citizens where teachers or clergy would instill knowledge from experts into the young. In many cases, the schools were run by the government, but some were formed by groups of parents. Participation in a community school was typically not compulsory, and many families chose not to participate.

In the mid-1800s in the United States, following a European trend, the creep of compulsory attendance in government schools slowly became a reality for elementary-aged students. By 1910, attendance in government schools was compulsory in every state, with religious school attendance as the lone exemption, and even that was not allowed in every state.

In 1890, having aged out of compulsory attendance, only about 7 percent of US teens were enrolled in a public high school. Most teens were employed full-time or in apprenticeships. A government push to build high schools in every community meant that enrollment was 32 percent by 1920, and it continued to grow until attendance became compulsory after World War II.

Throughout the 1800s and 1900s, the new experiment of compulsory attendance was met with a great deal of resistance from families that wanted something different for their children. Private and religious schools fought for legal status and became more numerous over the years. Some families did not enroll their children and faced school officials if confronted. The modern homeschool movement began in the 1950s, and, state by state, families took back their parental right to direct their children's educations. Homeschooling once again began to grow. Today, parent-directed home education is legal throughout the United States and in several other countries.

Many of today's parents do not realize that the public school system as we know it is only a recent experiment and that they are the ones to return to the tried-and-true roots of education. As in previous generations, parents work hard to help their children excel in their education and ensure success by using their whole world in this quest. While most families today no longer work the land and have businesses in their homes that they can employ their children in, they now have public libraries and the internet.

Today's homeschooling families face previously unknown challenges. Instead of having only one book, they can choose from millions. Instead of having a neighbor only a mile away (only an hour's walk round-trip) to teach children their sums, parents now have hundreds of expensive curriculum options, all proclaiming that their curriculum is "The Best" and the only one that will really work. Instead of being isolated and wishing they had parenting advice, today's parents deal with many other highly competitive parents proclaiming how gifted their child is, causing feelings of shame for the parent whose child is only at grade level or struggling with a subject, let alone one with special educational needs. Instead of being grateful for a quiet hour in the evening to sit with a child and read, today's parents are often wracked with guilt over not spending five hours a day sitting with each child teaching them one-on-one under the misguided memories of their own education. Instead of being thankful for a once-a-month market day where children could go into town and play with children other than their siblings, today's parents often feel guilty that their children do not have a healthy friendship with many other children their age.

But they also have a powerful resource that can combat every one of these challenges.

The public library! A natural ally located in almost every town, public libraries share the desire to help children excel in their education. As suppliers of resources for lifelong learners, librarians are called on to hold storytimes for 2-year-olds and book clubs for 10-year-olds. They have collections of special interest books for the local clubs, online access to free resources, and classes for those who want to learn special skills. They provide places for people to come to use a computer or pick up a book about almost anything to borrow where it is quiet and safe. Users of the library do not have to be wealthy; they only need to want to learn.

As homeschooling has continued to gain popularity, more and more libraries have begun to offer specialized services for homeschooling families. In 2001, thinking synergistically and being aware of a relatively large local population of homeschoolers, the Johnsburg Public Library in Johnsburg, Illinois, decided to leap. With a $55,000 grant of federal Library Services and Technology Act (LSTA) funds, the library purchased popular curricula, science equipment and kits, and a wealth of manipulatives chosen by a homeschooler for homeschoolers.

I am pleased to say these many years later that the Johnsburg Library continues to be a destination library, an often used resource for homeschoolers. New homeschoolers, anxious to hold, examine, and try materials, want to check out materials so they can try before they buy. Experienced homeschoolers love to drop in and borrow a microscope or some chemistry glassware for six weeks or know that they do not need to buy a fraction game when they get to that unit. They love the large collection of math literature (picture books) and, of course, the books about homeschooling spanning the wide variety of educational philosophies, learning styles, and experience levels. There are materials for a wide variety of religious backgrounds. There is something for everyone.

Keeping the collection current to the ever-evolving technological and pedagogical changes has kept the Johnsburg Library staff on their toes for several decades. New curriculum publishers come into and old publishers fall out of favor. Through it all, we have maintained that the collection would have something for everyone. If we add a book that features young earth theory, we add a book that features old earth theory. If we add a new book about the Charlotte Mason homeschooling philosophy, we make sure there are enough about Waldorf, Montessori, and Unschooling.

While we do not maintain a contact list of homeschoolers, to preserve their privacy, we have a guest book in the Homeschool Resource Center.

We ask only for their first name and their home state. We are delighted to see so many from across the United States come to visit, and the wonderful comments of support and encouragement that have been left for us in that little book are amazingly uplifting.

Our monthly workshops are designed to enrich and empower homeschoolers and do a great job advertising our collection. The crowd that gathers at our annual Used Curriculum Flea Market introduces more people to our little library than any other single event.

Libraries throughout the United States have contacted us over the years and inquired how and what we did. We have quite a bit of information on our web page and continue to love to field inquiries and host visits from librarians from other towns. One such visit was from the wonderful author of this book, Christina Giovannelli-Caputo. Christina shares my vision of mentoring other librarians and creating local homeschooling meccas of resources and support.

I hope the ideas Christina has gathered in this book support and encourage you on your quest to meet the unique needs of the homeschoolers in your community!

Kathy Wentz
Homeschool Liaison, Johnsburg Public Library

Preface

Dear Library Professional,

Thank you for advocating for library services to at home learners. I am glad you are here!

Library Services to Homeschoolers: A Guide has been written with the hope that fellow and future librarians will use this book to extend services to the growing and diverse at home learner audience. This book is meant to be an introduction to home education for library professionals, it is by no means the "end all and be all" comprehensive history of home education. My biggest piece of advice is to get to know the schooling community around your library and begin to foster connections. I have been in your shoes. I inherited homeschool programming at the library where I served in 2016. Sure, I knew of people that schooled from home but I did not know what exactly "homeschooling" meant and how the library fit into the equation of home education. In library school there was not a class on how to serve the home educated, and frankly I had no idea where to even start!

I looked at research from Homeschool Legal Defense Association (HSLDA.org) and National Home Education Research Institute (NHERI.org) along with various other homeschooling websites. I began exploring and sadly found a lack of information specifically for libraries and home education partnerships. The 2008 American Library Association (ALA) publication *Helping Homeschoolers in the Library* by Adrienne Furness was an invaluable guide for to me.

Yet, the educational landscape has changed quite a bit since 2008, especially with COVID-19. There has been a growing number of families transitioning to Alternative Education Methods (AEMs), which will be defined in the following chapters. Library services also have changed over the course of the COVID-19 pandemic. Libraries across the country have shifted to virtual programs, drive up services, craft kits, virtual reference, and so much more. As libraries and schools begin the road to transition back to in person programs and courses—some families are choosing to continue to school from home.

Furness saw a need in her community and in the library community and shared highly informative content, which inspired me to share what I learned with other professionals.

I began writing for Voices for Youth Advocates (VOYA) in 2017 with "Hanging with My Homies," a sole article that turned into a series. The series at VOYA, opened communication lines with library professionals around the country seeking advice on how to engage homeschoolers. In response, began publishing more of my research and I started a professional development group through Reaching Across Illinois Library System (RAILS), called "All Learners Welcome—Librarians Serving At Home Learners and Homeschool Families" (ALL). The ALL group met before COVID-19 in person and during COVID-19 virtually through Zoom. ALL has an email list to subscribe to and join: homeschool-join@list.railslibraries.info. I also began a Facebook group called "Librarians Serving At-Home Learners and Homeschoolers" and if you are on social media, connect with us! The networking at the ALL group led me to Kary Henry, a library professional from Deerfield Public Library, Deerfield, Illinois, who provided vast programming to homeschoolers. Kary and I teamed up to co-present at conferences in Illinois in 2019, Illinois Youth Services Institute (IYSI) and Reaching Forward. In 2020, I was recruited to teach for the Association for Library Service to Children, a division of the American Library Association, on "Serving At-Home Learners and Homeschoolers in the Public Library." In February of 2021, Bill Pardue, the digital services librarian from Arlington Heights Memorial Library, Arlington Heights, Illinois, and I presented at the North American Virtual Reference Online Conference, sharing our experience with our program "At-Home Parents Night In" and how we shifted our program that was previously an in-person offering to a virtual program due to COVID-19. I presented at YALSA 2021 on ALL are Welcome in the library, on engaging the schooling community. Librarians are crucial in fostering belonging in our communities. I saw a need to serve the home educated and advocated for unbiased services.

Chapter 1 begins with the historical roots of home education and origins of Compulsory Attendance in the United States. Chapter 2 explores the homeschool revolution, with leaders in this movement highlighted, such as John Holt, Dr. Raymond and Dorothy Moore, and John Taylor Gatto. After examining the historical context of education, chapter 3 examines home education in the twenty-first century. Currently, homeschooling is on the rise; Laws, advocacy groups, and COVID-19 all contributing to the surge. Chapter 4 looks at the various methods of home education. From home classrooms to travelschooling in recreational vehicles, traditional schooling to unschooling, and anywhere in between- families are unique in education methodologies and philosophies. The must read for librarians is chapter 5. This is where we dive deep into homeschool programming. Learn how public libraries can help parents and caregivers instruct their children by providing a place, materials, programs and so much more! In chapter 6, we explore many ways the library can provide outreach opportunities with local homeschooling groups, that foster community engagement. Chapter 7 looks at the growing diversity in home education. The final chapter peers into the future of home education, which will help librarians prepare for the needs of future homeschooling families.

Challenging the status quo of mainstream educational practices may be misunderstood by fellow librarians, administration, and even patrons. The likelihood is, you will be met with resistance, at some point or another. But I can guarantee you there are at home learners and homeschoolers in the community where you serve, and your advocacy is deeply needed. This journey may be taxing, it may be frustrating, but I promise you it will be so rewarding.

Is there a library system in your state that offers an option to begin a group or chapter for ALL? The learning community will benefit from the collaboration between innovative librarians like you! I would love to hear from you - my personal email is Christina.g.caputo@gmail.com

Happy reading!

Acknowledgments

Dominick, Rocco, Analisa, and Anthony,
 Thank you for the beautiful blessing of being your first and most important teacher. The four of you are my greatest achievements.

Nick,
 Per sempre, mi amore.

Momo and Nonno,
 Thank you for always believing in me and the gift of my MLIS.

My colleagues,
 Pat, thank you for taking the leap to programming for homeschoolers with me. Beloved Tina, thank you for seeing a need in the homeschooling community to serve. Kary, thank you for advocating with me. Bill, thank you for engaging the homeschooling community and always showing up (DSP). Kathy, thank you for paving the way for all of us who came after. RoseMary, thank you for the countless hours of editing and guidance.

The librarians,
 Thank you for being an inspiration to me and others for serving the homeschool communities.

Introduction

The research for this book is being compiled during the coronavirus disease 2019, abbreviated as COVID-19, pandemic. Currently, as the COVID-19 pandemic rages, families are taking control of their child's education, ascertaining this book is more important than ever for the future of library services to youth. Education, the way we knew it, is altering, evolving, and changing. As the future looms and technology progresses, the educational system cannot remain stagnant. It will not remain stagnant. Families will not remain stagnant. Youth learning cannot remain stagnant. And library services cannot remain stagnant.

During COVID-19, the education system has been thrust into the spotlight. Families are exploring alternative educational options for youth, as many brick-and-mortar schools have turned virtual. Remote schooling is working for some families, in-person learning is working for others, while additional families seek alternative schooling options. Micro schools and pods are popping up in communities, forest schools are erupting, and private schools are fielding calls for in-person enrollment. Also, there is the long-silent homeschooling population that continues educating uninterrupted. Many new "to homeschool" families are leaning on the veteran homeschoolers and groups for support, ideas, and encouragement. As for the libraries and librarians, they are, as they always have been, waiting to serve the communities.

The US Department of Education's Center for Educational Statistics (NCES) published *Homeschooling in the United States: Results from the 2012 and 2016 Parent and Family Involvement Survey* (PFI-NHES: 2012 and 2016), in which 70 percent of homeschooled parents cite the public library as their most valued resource.[1] The survey provides a random sampling of ages 5–17 of the entire American population. This sampling of families also answered a variety of queries about demographics and levels of parental education. The survey responses were compiled from 14,075 families, which included 552 self-reported and -identified homeschool families. From the reported survey results, researchers were able to make estimations on the American homeschooled population. The studies exclude students enrolled in a public or private school for more than 25 hours per week and those homeschooled due to temporary illness.

There are no hard and fast numbers or exact data for the home-educated youth in America. That is because, as we will learn, not all states have the same regulations for recording, registering, and homeschooling. More information on the survey and the compilation of PFI data and opinion polls are available for download through the NCES National Household Education Surveys Program website at https://nces.ed.gov/nhes/dataproducts.

In March 2020, many governments worldwide shut down the traditional educational walls of institutions to cease the spread of COVID-19. Over 190 countries closed schools and universities in response, some moving classes online, affecting over 1.5 billion children and youth. The United Nations Educational Scientific Cultural Organization (UNESCO) estimates that over 91 percent of students globally have been affected by school closures and learning from home.[2]

Currently, the *at-home* learner population is steadily on the rise worldwide. There is a quickly growing need for resources, instruction, and support from the public library. The 2020–2021 academic year looked quite different from previous years. Education departments from every state in America released proposals for safety guidelines. Each local school district had the authority and flexibility to reopen the schools with remote, hybrid, or in-person learning. Many of the requirements and suggestions were dependent on how the state contained the spread of COVID-19.

The safety protocols continued into the 2021-2022 school year as COVID-19 raged on. The CDC (Centers for Disease Control) updated school guidance in August of 2021, with universal masking regardless of vaccination status. To slow the transmission rate of the highly contagious Delta variant of COVID-19, it was recommended to mask and maintain 3 feet physical distancing between students in the classroom. Fall of 2021 brought youth masking and teacher vaccination mandates nationwide, which were highly visible in the mainstream media. School protocols varied by state, were flux and hotly debated from the political left through the political right.

Reference questions on homeschooling and at home learning continued (and continue to) bombard my email, voicemail, and network conversations. It is my goal, for the library to be the "GO-TO" for families seeking information on alternative education methods.

Home education is not a new or trendy movement. Homeschooling has long, deep roots in the United States and has been an educational option available for families. The home education numbers were steadily increasing before COVID-19, and skyrocketed during the 2020/2021 school year. Families and caregivers have continuously been educating their children, and historically homeschooling has been in each community the library serves. Families around the country are rethinking what education looks like and seeking alternative education methods (AEMs).

As the at-home learner population numbers steadily grow, the need for specialized library services, instruction, and support also has grown. The at-home learning and homeschool community needs the sustenance of the library and librarians. Before libraries can serve this specialized population, there must be an understanding of the educational history, which we will explore in chapter 1. The following chapters will explore the need to serve all learners at the library and the educational disparities, legalities, education reform, and the homeschooling revolution. COVID-19 has altered the way the populace lives and learns. We will explore how libraries need to respond to the education crisis and AEMs that are possibly present in the communities. Once we cover what the library needs to understand for focused and narrowed services for the at-home learner and homeschooler, in the final chapters, we will conclude with programming recommendations and look to the future of amenities.

Historically, the public library has been an extension of learning in partnership with schools. As the tides turn and more youth are at-home learners, libraries must make connections with the home-educated, including at-home learners. The homeschooled student will have different informational needs than those of a traditional student. The at-home learner will have a different informational need than that of an in-person student. The rapidly increasing number of at-home learners is a challenge and an opportunity for public librarians. There is a desperate need for the public library to open communication lines with the home-educated community. The library houses invaluable resources that are high in demand by the homeschoolers. The comprehensive milieu of the public library's collection, knowledgeable staff, educational programs, and innovative spaces has endless engagement possibilities.

So settle on in, fellow librarian. You are very much needed. The educational system needs you now, more than ever, to find creative ways to serve the youth of tomorrow. We are in for one wild and incredible ride!

Notes

1. J. Redford, D. Battle, and S. Bielick, *Homeschooling in the United States: 2012* (Washington, DC: National Center for Education Statistics, Institute of Education Sciences, US Department of Education, 2017).

2. UNESCO, "Global Education Collation: #Learning Never Stops," https://en.unesco.org/covid19/educationresponse/globalcoalition.

CHAPTER ONE

~

History of Homeschooling

The library is a cornerstone to the educational community, and public libraries must foster and build relationships with at-home learners. The educational landscape is in transition. While the historical context of education will remain unchanged, the future of schooling continues to evolve. Schooling diversity has been growing quietly for years.

Early American history has laid the groundwork for today's educational system—the origin of home education—teaching and learning dates to the beginning of time. The first child born to the first parents was home educated. The parents taught the child because there was no formalized educational system established.

The education model that is widely practiced and familiar to many, is merely one hundred years old (as of 2021). Home education is far older! Ever heard of the saying, "Parents are a child's first teacher?" The public domain document "Helping Your Child Succeed in School" by the US Department of Education references the quote by stating, "As our children's first and most important teacher, it is important that all parents build and keep strong ties to our children's schools. When parents and families are involved in their children's schools, the children do better and have better feelings about going to school."[1] Essentially, the interpretation of this—that it is beneficial and essential to have parents and caregivers involved in the learner's schooling—includes but is not limited to the learner's first teacher. Education begins in the home. As psychologist Alice Sterling Honig said, "Family is the first school for young children. And parents are powerful models."

Librarians have long supported the parent-as-the-first-teacher philosophy. In 2004, Every Child Ready to Read (ECRR) was developed. The Association for Library Service to Children (ALSC) and the Public Library Association (PLA) determined that public and community libraries influence and significantly impact early learning. The library supports early literacy in story times, programs for the young child, and parental support. "If the primary adults in a child's life can learn more about the importance of early literacy and how to nurture pre-reading skills at home, the effect of library efforts can be multiplied many times."[2] There is a natural fit for librarians and libraries to support families and early literacies, which acknowledges caregivers as a young child's most significant influence and teacher. In the "olden days," a parent was the teacher, and the teacher was the parent. Mother, father, and extended family taught the child/ren.

Formalized mass and common schooling are a new concept in the history of the Americas, and the following is research on home and formalized education. Interestingly, much of the research and writings on the American history of education begins in the 17th century. While settlers migrated to the "new land" and the first school buildings were erected during the same time, education spans far beyond. The following research aims to establish and compile a historical context for home education and the newer common and mass education.

The exact date of civilization in the Americas is unknown. A recent discovery followed by research from the Chiquihuite Cave in Mexico's northwest region provides evidence that humans may have inhabited the Americas earlier than believed. Stone objects were discovered deep inside the barren and remote Chiquihuite Cave, suggesting human occupancy and rewriting the Americas' history. A study published by the journal *Nature* suggests human life in North America about 30,000 years ago.[3] This is approximately double what was estimated before this study. This topic has been hotly debated for over a century, according to *National Geographic*.[4] These findings of life—human remains—are thought to have traveled from Siberia to the Americas through the Bering Strait, searching for game. They migrated to South America through the Isthmus of Panama.[5] This research has not been written to spark a debate or undermine experts but merely to establish that home education has been occurring in previous and ancient generations for thousands of years.

Researchers have found evidence dating thousands of years ago of human life before the colonization of the Americas. To begin a population and grow to generations, naturally, there was procreation. We are not sure exactly how children learned or if there is detailed proof of proper schooling; it is assumed that the elders taught the youth. Evidence of a "hunter and gatherer" community emerged around 11,000 BP (before present) that learned to hunt and gather from someone or something.

As time went on and people, families, and communities evolved, there was more formal schooling. While this chapter focuses on the Americas' home education history, there was teaching and learning happening in populations globally. The ancient Egyptians developed hieroglyphics, a written language, and developed a form of literacy, to name one. While in these ancient civilizations there were no school buildings per se, ancient adolescents learned through parents, scholars, and priests. During this same era, the first library in the world was developed—the Library of Alexandria. With the advancement and development of the first library, there was a way to record knowledge and expand learning. Native American academic and activist Dr. Henrietta Whiteman-Mann said, "Contrary to popular belief, education—the transmission and acquisition of knowledge and skills—did not come to the North American continent on the Nina, Pinta, and Santa Maria. We Native Americans have educated our youth through a rich and oral tradition."

However, teaching and learning was an oral custom to the native peoples who inhabited the Americas. Historians and researchers have estimated the population of indigenous Americans in America north of Mexico before 1492, and the estimations greatly vary. William M. Denevan writes that "the discovery of America was followed by possibly the greatest demographic disaster in the history of the world." Research by some scholars provides population estimates of the pre-contact Americas as high as 112 million in 1492, while others estimate the population to have been as low as 8 million. Nevertheless, the native population declined to less than 6 million by 1650.[6]

Before the Europeans traveled to the Americas, Native American Indian tribes developed an effective aboriginal/indigenous educational system. The National Museum of the American Indian says, "Elders in each generation teach the next generation their values, traditions, and beliefs through their own tribal languages, social practices, arts, music, ceremonies, and customs."[7] The schooling was formed by dispersing learned skills, such as knowledge, morals, and temperaments, to the following generations of youth. The Native American community supported and valued education, ensuring that both genders had equal access to learning. Boys were instructed by their fathers and male elders. Girls were taught by their mothers and female elders. The whole community taught the youth of Native American Indian/indigenous American tribes, as everyone in the tribe had significant teachings to pass on; nevertheless, the youth's family was the most influential. As stated in American Education by Urban and Wagoner, "The rearing of children was everyone's concern, for they understood that the life of the tribe—the life of "the people"—could be preserved and extended only for as long as the rising generations followed the ways of the old."[8]

The Native American Indian or indigenous American tribes and their history began long before the 15th century. There is a strong probability that the people native to the Americas did not speak the English language; it was a learned language from European colonization. It was many years until the Americas developed a similar written, recorded literacy, at least, that we know. In 1821, Sequoyah, a Cherokee man, developed the spoken language's written form, allowing for the oral Cherokee history to be recorded. Sequoyah worked for 12 years to develop an alphabet of 85 symbols representing consonant and vowel sounds. The written language was approved in 1825 by Cherokee chiefs. This linguistic code made it possible for widespread literacy to the Cherokee people following the alphabet's adoption.

The 15th-century European exploration of the world and the New World was sparked by trade. Explorers immigrated to and settled within the new 13 colonies in the Americas. With the 17th-century settlers also came European views and ways. Youth education was ingrained within the home, a shared similarity to the native people of the Americas. As the young nation's population grew, so did the everyday jobs essential for existence in the new land. Everyone, youth included, regardless of their gender, all had a part to play in the survival on the home front. Young men often learned how to raise and care for livestock, to build, to shape tools, and to labor in the fields. Young women often learned how to make

Figure 1.1. "Sequoyah, Cherokee inventor, by C.B. King, ca. 1836." Library of Congress, LC-DIG-pga-07569.

clothes, cook, and care for the home and younger siblings. These were the main foundations of learning in the early days of America.[9]

The New World's educational arrangement had ties to and origins in the Protestant Reformation, which believed schooling is necessary for all people to comprehend Scripture. It was not long after the Mayflower settlers of 1609 that educational institutions were being formed. As the populations grew in the early colonies, public education methodologies also grew.

In April 1635, the Boston Latin School was founded and currently holds the title of the oldest public school in the United States of America. According to the Boston Latin School (BLS.org), it was founded by the town of Boston (Massachusetts) to replicate the Free Grammar School of Boston, England. Public schooling in 1635 had a different connotation of—or how we define—today's public schooling; however, it was supported by taxes. The BLS was free for males, regardless of class, and the curriculum focused on the humanities. The first courses of BLS were held in the homes of the school masters until completion of the schoolhouse in 1645.

The Boston Latin School sparked the beginning of public, tax-funded education. In 1642 the Massachusetts Act was passed. The first law in the New World stated that close relatives were accountable for youth's basic

Figure 1.2. Boston Latin School Plaque. Daderot.

schooling. The ideology was to create good moral citizens that could read and abide by the laws. In 1647, Massachusetts approved the "Old Deluder Satan Act." The 1647 act placed the groundwork for communal public schooling in America.

The Old Deluder Satan Act of 1647 obligated every area (town or village) of 50 families or more to fund and offer a teacher education for the area's youth. Areas of 100 families or more were then obligated to support a grammar/elementary school (also called town school) to prepare youth to attend Harvard College.

Harvard is the oldest higher education institution in the United States. It was established and founded in 1636 by ballot of the "Great and General Court of the Massachusetts Bay Colony," according to Harvard's website (Harvard.edu). Harvard was named after the college's first funding supporter, John Harvard. The acts recognize numerous public education principles, both elementary and high school, and presently hold that basic education is a fundamental right. "The state can require communities to raise and expend local funds for schools, that day-to-day responsibility for the operation of schools rests at the local level, and that schools are to be organized in levels separating elementary from secondary education."[10]

Widespread community schooling was sluggish to grow during this time. Hence, the 1647 mandate. Other New England colonies followed suit and adopted similar laws, all but Rhode Island. However, the early colonial residents of the United States often settled quite far apart. The distance between homes and towns created educational difficulties, and youth were needed to help at home. Eventually, the population grew, and towns could support and fund area schools. Yet going to school was costly for families. Most schools were tuition based, and if the school happened to be free, there was no labor or help at home. According to sociologist Sara Lawrence Lightfoot, "There must be a profound recognition that parents are the first teachers, and that education begins before formal schooling and is deeply rooted in the values, traditions, and norm[s] of family and culture."

By the end of the 1700s, many boys in colonial America attended "dame schools," characterized by Brittanica.com as small private schools for young children run by women. They existed in England possibly before the 16th century in both towns and rural areas and survived into the 19th century. The school was frequently in the teacher's home, in which the children were taught the alphabet and some reading from the New Testament and given household chores." Dame schools were defined as a school influenced by the English model of home instruction for small groups of children usually led by a woman in her home (Monaghan, 1988). Dame schools are the early

Figure 1.3. The Dame School. David Wilkie.

one-room schoolhouses and precursors to preschools of today. The foundation of dame schools grew and formed in the kitchens of older women in the town. An important development at this time, it established women as teachers in colonial America.

Public schools did not mean universal. During this time, a child's gender determined their level of schooling. The early preschools' main emphasis was to get the males ready for admission to the town (elementary schools of today) schools. Until the 19th century, girls were not allowed admittance.[11] Females were eventually admitted to the elementary town schools. Typically, the girls attended at alternative times or when boys were not in attendance, such as summer or winter. It was not until 1972 when the Boston Latin School became coeducational.

The educational model in colonial times was built and fueled by religion. As time went on, the populations and communities grew, and it became customary for the youth to attend school. The schooling method was up to the parents, just as it is in modern times. The New World continued to expand, as did education. While the methodologies about education were changing, the role of the government increased in the institution of education.

Horace Mann is often referred to as "The Father of the Common School Movement." He was the leading advocate of education restructure reform in historical America. Mann laid the groundwork for the common school movement, a free, nonreligious, public organization. Mann argued the

Figure 1.4. Horace Mann, 1850. Southworth and Hawes.

common school purpose was to attain and improve Americans' ethical and financial status.

Mann was a prominent political leader of the Whig Party and in 1837 was appointed as secretary of the Massachusetts Board of Education. From his position, he advocated for the common school and education as social refurbishment. The ideology that the common school would be universal among all economic class youth avoid lawlessness, improve public engagement, and instruct ethical-moral behavior. Youth were to be taught in the ways, stories, and morals of the Bible, while not to be persuaded to a religious denomination in the Common School method. Soon Mann's educational model expanded beyond the borders of Massachusetts. He began the *Common School Journal* and published books on his work.

Mann faced differing viewpoints on his mission and work. Some felt his work and universal schooling advocacy paved the way for allowing differing social classes to succeed. It was believed in this viewpoint that the Common School allowed for deservingness to trump birthright. While others felt the Common School movement was a form of social control with Protestant views, the most malleable and moldable members of society were indoctrinated to learn the same curriculum.

Public education was not the only educational system being built in the Americas. Concurrent with the establishment and surge of the 13 colonies, in 1606, Franciscan Catholic Missionaries established a school in current St. Augustine, Florida.[12] Many of the public schools established by the settlers were heavily Protestant and taught Protestant views. As the Catholic population began to grow, so did the need for Catholic schools. There was a surge in Catholic missionaries and Catholic immigrants to the New World. New Catholic immigrants began to seek out alternative educational options, including Catholic parochial schools.

Compulsory Attendance Acts

More states began following Massachusetts' educational lead by employing compulsory attendance laws. Compulsory attendance is the age requirement, length of the school year, enrollment necessities, enforcement, and truancy requirements set forth for the schools by the state. Eventually, each state in the new nation had compulsory attendance laws put into practice. While universal education and literacy were compulsory attendance's main goals, it was also placed into action to reject the prevalent common youth labor work of the 19th and early 20th centuries.

Mississippi was the last state to join in the compulsory attendance laws in 1918. During the influenza pandemic of 1918–1919, many cities nationwide employed and implemented community mitigation strategies, the most common being school closures. Three heavily populated cities chose not to close public schools, arguing youth were safer in schools. It is important to note the atypical actions of New York City, Chicago, and New Haven "viewed keeping schools open not as an abdication of public health responsibility, but as an opportunity to implement the public health strategies of school medical inspection and intensified disease surveillance." There were many changes in schooling during this time.[13]

Compulsory attendance's original model in the Americas is the prototype grounded in universal "attendance" in school. According to Augustina Reyes, author of *Compulsory School Attendance: The New American Crime*, the prototype presumed formal schooling was required for "social progress and served as a frame for early compulsory school attendance laws." Consider the infusion of immigrants during the post-1860 period and following World Wars I and II.[14] The American educational model that we know today is based upon the Americanization Movement. The American population soared with immigrants in the late nineteenth and early twentieth century. Around twenty-three million Europeans immigrated to the US and by 1910 15 percent of the population was immigrants. Detroit, New York, and Los Angeles all established programs to assimilate the foreign born. The nation utilized compulsory education laws to Americanize immigrant youth. The compulsory attendance laws were a way for the states to introduce mainstream standards. Americans believed in the power of schooling to transform all kinds of people into citizens.

Compulsory attendance laws were ratified, and the government enforced them to safeguard youth in all socioeconomic classes and ensure they received a basic, "common" education. The Progressive reformers were active in America from 1894–1915 and believed education would conform youth to be active and productive citizens. Many immigrant teens and youth from working-class families did not attend high school or university during this time; they needed to work to help support the family. The common education was to teach the youth proper American values. While the intention of universal public education was good, not all youth were educated in the same manner.

During this same period, the federal government required special schools created for the Native American Indian youth. Along with schools for immigrant youth, these schools were to assimilate them to the newfound American White culture. The Library of Congress Digital Collection "America At Work" states, "European models of schooling influenced U.S. schools in the late 1800s, most notably the German kindergartens and industrial schools. The first kindergarten was established in Germany in 1837 and in the U.S. in 1856."

It became the American Dream, that an education catapults people to a different level of society with greater earning potential. Over time, education was not seen as a privilege but as a fundamental right. The words of the Northwest Ordinance are instructive. Article III reads, in part: "Religion, morality, and knowledge being necessary to good government and the happiness of mankind, schools and the means of education shall forever be encouraged." Please note the order of priority: religion, morality, and knowledge.[15]

Take the modern-day educational arena, for example. Perhaps most readers (of this book) have taken a role in traditional education, whether it be student, teacher, librarian, and so on. There is a societal and social ambivalence today when it comes to alternative education methods (AEMs). Not because we do not want to learn more about them, but because we have been schooled in a different model. Schooling diversity is a growing global trend.

We are committed to schooling our children, yet we tend to reject that schooling's objectives. Long before the service state came into existence with the New Deal in the 1930s, the states and the nation were committed to supplying schooling to accomplish such education. Although the states have assumed the major burden of their citizens' formal education, the national commitment was evidenced even before the birth of the United States in the provisions of the Northwest Ordinance. The American educational system became an assumed right.

While education is assumed as an American birthright, there is no federal order on compulsory attendance. The Constitution prohibits a federal mandate requiring universal compulsory attendance. The absence of the constitutional obligation for education then falls to the states to provide an education for its people, which is stated in the Tenth Amendment of the US Constitution: "The powers not delegated to the United States by the Constitution, nor prohibited by it to the States, are reserved to the States respectively, or to the people." The federal umbrella may require some educational mandates under the Constitution, for example, the General Welfare Clause, which allows for federal interventions. Formal schooling is not a "right" under the US Constitution; states have assumed the educational responsibility. Hence, there are discrepancies in the level of education in regulations among the states. The discrepancies require us to rethink the education model as we know it.

Notes

1. US Department of Education, Office of Communications and Outreach, "Helping Your Child Succeed in School" (Washington, DC, 2005).

2. Public Library Association and Association for Library Service to Children, "Every Child Ready to Read," American Library Association, http://everychildready toread.org.

3. C. F. Ardelean et al., "Evidence of Human Occupation in Mexico around the Last Glacial Maximum," *Nature* 584, no. 7819 (2020): 87–92, https://doi.org/10.1038/s41586-020-2509-0.

4. Kristin Romney, "Surprise Cave Discoveries May Double the Time People Lived in the Americas," *National Geographic*, July 2020, https://www.nationalgeographic.com/history/2020/07/surprise-chiquihuite-cave-discovery-mexico-double-peopling-americas.

5. P. A. Franklin, *Indians of North America: The Eight Cultural Areas and How Their Inhabitants Lived before the Coming of Whites* (New York, NY: David McKay, 1979).

6. William M. Denevan, ed., *The Native Population of the Americas in 1492* (Madison, WI: University of Wisconsin, 1992).

7. National Museum of the American Indian, Smithsonian, "Transforming Teaching and Learning about Native Americans," https://americanindian.si.edu/nk360.

8. W. J. Urban and J. L. Wagoner, *American Education: A History*, third ed. (New York, NY: McGraw-Hill Companies, 2004).

9. E. J. Monaghan, "Literacy Instruction and Gender in Colonial New England," *American Quarterly* 40 (1988): 18–41.

10. John R. Vile, David L. Hudson, and David Schultz, *Encyclopedia of the First Amendment* (Washington, DC: CQ Press, 2009).

11. C. Riordan, *Girls and Boys in School: Together or Separate?* (New York, NY: Teachers College Press, 1990).

12. "Pope's Visit Spotlights U.S. Catholic School Revival through Embracing Reform," The 74, September 24, 2015, https://www.the74million.org/article/popes-visit-spotlights-us-catholic-school-revival-through-embracing-reform/.

13. Alexandra Minna Stern et al., "'Better Off in School': School Medical Inspection as a Public Health Strategy during the 1918–1919 Influenza Pandemic in the United States," *Public Health Reports* 125, no. 3 (2010): 63–70, https://doi.org/10.1177/00333549101250S309.

14. Reyes, Augustina. *Compulsory School Attendance: The New American Crime.* Education Sciences. March 16, 2020. https://files.eric.ed.gov/fulltext/EJ1250513.pdf.

15. "Northwest Ordinance (1787)," ourdocuments.gov, https://www.ourdocuments.gov/doc.php?flash=false&doc=8.

CHAPTER TWO

Homeschool Revolution

As the twentieth century approached, more youth attended brick-and-mortar schools than ever before in the young nation. It became commonplace to attend elementary school, and more youth began achieving a high school education. During the rapid influx of immigrants coming to America, political leaders were candid about the result to stakeholders. The educational paradigm was shifting.

Author Robert Slawson recounts in his 2005 book *Department of Education Battle, 1918-1932 Public Schools, Catholic Schools, and the Social Order* a collaboration between Columbia University's Teachers College and the National Education Association (NEA). This collaboration became known as "The Education Trust" by the press and media. It set in motion a movement for national universal schooling and baseline of the US Department of Education. "The Education Trust" was composed of organizations that cultivated social and civil progressiveness, contributors- such as Harvard, Rockefeller, Carnegie, Stanford, University of Chicago, and the National Education Association. Not as commonly known, "The Education Trust" was also supported by the Southern Jurisdiction of Scottish Rite Masonry (Masons) and the Ku Klux Klan (KKK). For further reading on the KKK's impact in public education, I recommend *The Ku Klux Klan in the City, 1915-1930*, by Kenneth Jackson and *Department of Education Battle, 1918-1932 Public Schools, Catholic Schools, and the Social Order 1918-1932 Public Schools, Catholic Schools, and the Social Order* by Robert Slawson.

18 ~ Chapter Two

Figure 2.1.   Overcrowded Black School, 1917. Lewis Hine.

The Masons, KKK and Oregon Democratic gubernatorial candidate Walter M. Pierce joined forces to advocate and sponsor, the Oregon School Bill, also known as The Oregon Compulsory Attendance Act of 1922. The Act required that *all* Oregon youth attend public school, or the family would face hefty fines and potential jail time.

During this time the KKK pushed for national education reform, and supported the 1923 Smith Towner Bill, which created a US Department of Education. The KKK expanded reach to squash school choice and drafted a bill by petition in the state of Washington, called Washington Compulsory Schooling Initiative, aka Initiative 49 in 1924. The KKK declared public schools were "nurseries of democracy," and youth in private schools were trained to be devoted to "foreign institutions" and not loyal to the United States. The purpose of both the 1922 Act and the 1924 bill, was to eradicate private schools and mandate public schooling.

In a legal battle that came to a climax during the 1925 US Supreme Court case, Pierce v. Society of Sisters, established that mandated public schooling was unconstitutional. *Pierce v. Society of Sisters* is highlighted in chapter 3.[1]

Public schooling was gaining popularity, however not all public schools were universally equal. African American youth were required to attend segregated classes and schools with fewer resources. The standard funding for segregated schools was dependent on the state and was typically nominal. Northern states had better schools with higher attendance rates for African American children than the Southern states. The Jim Crow laws passed after the Civil War restricted people of colors' usage of public spaces, including (but not limited to) schools. There were White schools, and then there were Black schools, which were sadly far inferior.

Unfortunately, Black youth often went to school in dilapidated, unheated buildings with overcrowded classrooms and grossly lesser paid teachers. Typically, the Black youth used White school discards—old, worn-out textbooks, desks, and other materials. In state after state, the amount of funding provided to public schools depended on the students' race. Beaufort County, South Carolina, for instance, spent $40.68 per White pupil and only $5.95 per Black pupil in 1910. The average value of a school building for White students was $30,056 that year, while the average value of a Black school was $3,953—a dramatically lesser amount.[2]

Often, Black youth were working and not able to attend schools until later in the fall. Ann Pointer, who attended a two-room school in Macon County, Georgia, in the 1930s, remembered that "one teacher taught [grades] one through three, the other taught four through six. And we could not go to school until October. . . . And you know why? Because Mr. Childer's cotton had to be picked and gathered before the black children went to school." In some cases, Black students attended school for only a few days a week or a few months a year.[3]

Due to the inferiority of the education the Black youth received in public schools, communities rallied together to supplement the education of Black youth. Elders in the community and church would hold informal classes to teach the youth of their experience with slavery and share African Americans' ancestorial stories and achievements. Many public schools disregarded or misrepresented Black history within the curricula. The oral tradition of stories shared by the elders preserved the African American people's cultural and racial pride.

In current times, some Black families are grasping control of their child's education through homeschooling in a freedom affirmation from systemic schooling. There is research that supports systemic racism can be rooted in public school curricula and, sadly, schools themselves, which has been evident by the disciplinary disparities demonstrated in numerous studies.[4] The advocacy work for Black educational freedom was propelled by Black ancestors more than a century ago.

One of the most significant education law cases is *Brown v. Board of Education*, from 1954. This case is extremely important. It sets a precedent and reiterates that "separate is not equal." The Supreme Court unanimously ruled that it is unconstitutional to separate youth by race in public schools. The racial segregation of youth in public schools violated the Equal Protection Clause of the Fourteenth Amendment.[5] While *Brown* did not desegregate schools in America fully, it was one of the greatest Supreme Court decisions of the 20th century, as it placed the Constitution on the side of racial equality and sparked the civil rights movement.

Modern Homeschooling

The homeschooling community has long and deep roots in the Americas, as the previous chapter has established. Once the advent of compulsory education and public education became commonplace, homeschooling flew under the radar. Homeschooling has been shaped by a diverse group of people in this country.

The 1970s

John Holt was a vocal critic of public education in America. He was a significant advocate for home education in the 1970s and 1980s and was considered the "Father of Homeschooling." Holt was a teacher and author. In 1964, his first book, *How Children Fail*, sparked great debate. In it, he argued compulsory education defeats a youth's natural curiosity and replaces it with insecurity and a scared desire to please the teacher. Holt said, "It's not that I feel that school is a good idea gone wrong, but a wrong idea from the word go. It's a nutty notion that we can have a place where nothing but learning happens, cut off from the rest of life."

In 1967, his second book, *How Children Learn*, compared compulsory schooling methods and informal home education methods. Holt's critiques and vocalness of the system of education were not popular with fellow educators. Eventually, he left the classroom after refusing to assess or test students. Holt went on to be a lecturer at Harvard Graduate School of Education and University of California, Berkeley. His views became radical, and he found himself as the voice of homeschooling in the 1970s after he published *Instead of Education: Ways to Help People Do Things Better* in 1976. Holt began the first homeschooling newsletter, "Growing Without Schooling," published from 1977–2001.

Holt worked tirelessly to build connections with marginalized schooling communities. In 1978, Holt appeared on the *Phil Donahue Show* with a homeschooling family and gained the mainstream media's attention. Holt's later years were spent in court securing the legal foundation for homeschooling today. The late Holt's website (www.johnholtGWS.com) is maintained by homeschool researcher and advocate, Pat Farenga. Farenga worked closely with Holt and published the "Growing Without School" newsletter. Farenga is the current president of JohnHoltGWS and a founding member of Alternatives to School (www.alternativestoschool.com).

According to Holt, a person has the fundamental right to express personal inner thoughts and learning while speaking them publicly under the First Amendment. "A person's freedom of learning is part of his freedom of thought, even more basic than his freedom of speech. If we take someone's right to decide what he will be curious about, we destroy his freedom of thought. We say, in effect, you must think not about what interests and concerns *you* but about what interests and concerns *us*." Holt goes on to say in *Escape from Childhood*, "There are very few people in the U.S. today (or perhaps anywhere, anytime) in *any* occupation, who could be trusted with the kind of power that schools give most teachers over their students. Schools seem to be among the most anti-democratic, most authoritarian, most destructive, and most dangerous institutions of modern society. No other institution does more harm or more lasting harm to more people or destroys so much of their curiosity, independence, trust, dignity, and sense of identity and worth."

Holt's strong opinion is what has gained him a following. The once-radical views were being heard and accepted by families, in turn growing homeschooling once again. As established, while homeschooling was not eradicated, it went under the radar after compulsory education became the norm. As homeschooling reformers became vocal on home education's benefits, the norm began to shift yet again. The once considered extremist views became valued and noticed.

Dr. Raymond Moore and his wife, Dorothy, are often considered the grandparents of homeschooling. Dr. Moore authored the book *Better Late than Early*, a catalyst in the modern homeschool movement. He was a former teacher, principal, and superintendent from California public schools, and his article in *Harper's Bazaar* in 1972 was the inspiration for his book. The catalyst for the article in *Harper's* was California's push for compulsory education to begin at 2 years and 9 months old. Moore opposed the proposal. The Moores established the Moore Foundation and the Moore Formula. Information from the Moorehomeschooling.com website says, "The Moore Academy is a branch of Moore Foundation, the homeschooling organization begun by Dr. Raymond and Dorothy Moore due to their education research done in the late 1960s and early 70s." In *School Can Wait*, Moore said, "Homeschool history tells of more than two centuries of home-teaching influence on American education, although it has been largely obscured by the drawn curtains of conventional bias."

Universities, according to the Moore website, "widely approve of the Moore Formula educational method." Dr. Moore has shared authorship on 35 textbooks for colleges on the method as well. The Moores are very well known for the "emphasis on the philosophy that children, especially boys, need individualized attention, chiefly between the ages of five and ten." The Moore Formula is based on the philosophy that "High success comes when close individual attention is paid to the needs of the student, following their interests, and allowing them to mature at their own rate, with emphasis on work (for pay), and service (in the home and the community) with these non-academic learning opportunities receiving equal time to book learning."

The modern homeschool movement took root in the 1970s and was led on the political left by John Holt and on the political right by Dr. Raymond Moore. It is also important to note that, before 1993, homeschooling was illegal in many states. There are 50 different homeschooling histories for the 50 diverse states, all varying in regulation, ease of installation, and policy. During the homeschool revolution, some states acted on the education policy alteration without judicial involvement. Some states added a statement to their bills, and other states had detailed homeschool rules. Current regulations of homeschooling vastly differ from state to state, with low to high regulations.

The 1980s

Milton Gaither called homeschooling in the 1980s "the changing of the guard." At the reemergence of home education, secular and religious homeschool advocates worked side by side to unite homeschooling at the national, state, and local levels. There were legal battles to be fought and alliances that strengthened the reform. Holt and the Moores laid the groundwork for the homeschool movement, but their leadership hold began to diminish by the end of the 1980s. Holt passed away in 1985. While his legacy lives on today, the homeschooling movement transitioned to Evangelical Christian. The mold did not fit Holt or the Moores, who were Seventh Day Adventists. The alliances that were formed began to crumble. The Moores called for unity within the homeschooling movement between secular and religious groups, but it was ineffective. However, as the Evangelical Christian homeschoolers rose, the new leaders of homeschooling became the Homeschool Legal Defense Association.

There was a rise of Evangelical Christian homeschooling groups after *Engel v. Vitale* on June 25, 1962, and *Abington School District v. Schempp*, on June 17, 1963—Supreme Court cases that made prayer and devotional reading in public schools unconstitutional. With the advent of those cases also came Homeschool Legal Defense Association (HSLDA) in 1983. HSLDA was formed by two homeschooling attorney fathers, Mike Harris and Mike Smith. The purpose was and is of HSLDA to provide legal representation for homeschooling families. As of 2021 HSLDA serves 100,000+ families, according to HSLDA.org, by providing "legal representation, educational consulting, practical resources, or grants for struggling families. Everything we do flows from our core mission of making homeschooling possible."

The homeschooling revolution exploded in the 1980s as more families began to explore alternative educational methodologies (AEMs). Educational control was the catalyst for the large reemergence of the home education movement. According to scholars Reese (1995) and Tyack (1974), the critical educational issues were forced by government control and parents' lack thereof.[6] Their work exposes two significant points. Families raged against the education machine, demanding to be heard and for school choice. At the same time, governments assumed expanding responsibility for social life[7] and diminished parents' influence and role.[8]

The 1990s

John Taylor Gatto, was a thirty-year veteran schoolteacher, who was named New York State Teacher of the Year and New York City Teacher of the Year mulitple times. In 1991, he wrote an article for the Wall Street Journal called "I Quit, I Think." He stated "government schooling is the most radical adventure in history" and he was "no longer willing to hurt children." In 1992, Gatto wrote a groundbreaking, thought-provoking radical book, *Dumbing Us Down: The Hidden Curriculum of Compulsory Schooling*. He also wrote *Weapons of Mass Instruction: A Schoolteacher's Journey Through the Dark World of Compulsory Schooling*, which calls compulsory education deliberatively destructive to all youth, especially Black youth. Gatto called for youth and families to break away from compulsory schooling indoctrinated in mainstream society. Through his work; publications and speaking, he rose in prominence, as an unschooling advocate. Gatto was adamant about deconstructing the public school system and demystifying the pedagogy of education. He said, "There isn't a right way to become educated; there are as many ways as fingerprints."

Gatto was appointed, Secretary of Education to the Libertarian Shadow Party in 1992. According to his website (johntaylorgatto.com), he traveled millions of miles in all 50 states and seven global countries, speaking on his

24   Chapter Two

Figure 2.2.   John Taylor Gatto. Kirbster.

platform prior to his death in 2018. One of his books is available on the Internet Archive, An Underground History of American Education, which can be accessed at https://archive.org/details/AnUndergroundHistoryOf AmericanEducationJohnTaylorGatto. By the middle of 1993, homeschooling was legal in all 50 states of America. The schooling methodology had come back full circle in a historical context. The homeschool population was growing.

Pedagogy is often a synonym for education and the science of education. Pedagogy derives from the Latin *pedagogues*. *Pedagogues* is Latin for a specialized group of slaves who walked a child to the tutor—a child leader: *pedo* for a child and *agogues* for the leader. The *pedagogues* slave would then enforce—the equivalent of a drill sergeant of today. Over time, the word evolved to pedagogy, and the original meaning was lost in the historical abyss. A common term to modern schooling, yet free men and women were never *pedagogues*.

Librarians are innovators and have been serving the homeschoolers in their communities faithfully. During the modern homeschool revolution, a library in Pennsylvania helped a 9-year-old youth (at the time) present preschool story times. The homeschooled youth worked alongside the librarian

THE PEDAGOGICAL SEMINARY.

Founded and Edited by G. STANLEY HALL.

WHAT IS PEDAGOGY?[1]

By G. STANLEY HALL.

The Greek pedagogue, from whom the term pedagogy was derived, led the boy to and from school, and was his keeper rather than his teacher. The word has expanded from its etymological meaning and is a general designation for the art of teaching. Twenty years ago the term was not held in honor in academic circles and others were preferred. Years ago a classical professor in a vivacious article declared that, in his mind, it was associated with pettifogging and was a word that he always tried to avoid, and thought its connotations vulgar. In many minds it is still associated with teaching in the primary grades and for college and university work had little meaning. In the designation of academic chairs the term "Education" was preferred and if pedagogy had a place it was thought to be chiefly in the normal schools. Its respectability and its scope, however, have steadily increased in recent years, till I think we may fairly say it should now include both didactics or the methods of teaching or imparting knowledge or instruction generally on the one hand—all those processes by which information is given—and on the other, education or development from within outward. Thus we may properly speak of the educational value of all instruction, and we are coming to see this varies much for different subjects of the curriculum. Education is more humanistic and evolutionary, and aims to unfold all the powers of the individual to their maximal maturity and strength and is essentially cultural; while teaching, learning, and didactics generally consist in transmitting knowl-

---

[1] Introductory lecture to the popular Saturday courses, given at Clark University, Saturday, September 30, 1905.

Figure 2.3. What is Pedagogy? G. Stanley Hall, 1905.

to choose stories, songs, and rhymes in the mid-1980s. Another library began focusing on services and programs for the home educated. Kings County Library System offered workshops and library tours to home-educated youth, packets to give to new homeschool families, and booklists. They also raised the bar by suggesting homeschooling training professional development for library staff. Kings County also participated in the Washington Homeschool Convention to become more visible to the homeschooling community.[9]

The homeschooling revolution has come a long way since reemerging in the 1970s. The storyline for home education has begun to be unfolded in previous and following chapters. In the 1970s, the estimated homeschooling population was between 10,000 and 20,000, and in the 40 to 50 years since, it has grown in great numbers. Before COVID-19, the National Center for Educational Statistics (NCES) estimated around 2 million youth were homeschooled. Growth rates have been calculated from 7 percent to 12 percent per annum.[10]

For librarians who serve the community, it is necessary to connect with all forms of schooling institutions. The NCES estimated 3.5 percent of all school-aged youth are homeschooled. Learning about your community local to the library will focus efforts on linking library resources to schools. Homeschooling has grown drastically over the years, with a vast diversity in schooling options and reasonings. There is often a misconception about high-performing or "good" school districts that there will be minimal schooling diversity. But, as we learned, there is not a one size fits all approach to schooling. Good school districts do not deter AEMs; people school in the method right for their family.

Sidebar 2.1

By learning about the community where I serve, I estimated the homeschooling numbers at 6 percent locally, 2.5 percent higher than the national average. The library administration asked why people would choose to homeschool in a "destination school district." It is simple. Every family has different schooling needs, each child learns differently, and education is not a universal form—it needs differentiation. It is called schooling diversity, to school outside of the norm.

Notes

1. Ben H. Britton et al, "Arguments on Behalf of Proponents of Initiative Measure Number Forty-Nine," filed on July 17, 1924, in the State of Washington Pamphlet for the November 5, 1924 election, compiled by Secretary of State J. Grant Hinkle (Olympia: Frank M. Lamborn, 1924), 5.

2. Anne Kelsey, "At Their Own Deliberate Speed: The Desegregation of the Public Schools in Beaufort County, South Carolina," PhD diss. (Clemson University, 2010), https://tigerprints.clemson.edu/cgi/viewcontent.cgi?article=1856&context=all_theses.

3. L. B. Osborne, *Miles to Go for Freedom: Segregation & Civil Rights in the Jim Crow Years* (New York, NY: Abrams Books for Young Readers, 2012).

4. D. Johns, "Disrupting Implicit Racial Bias and Other Forms of Discrimination to Improve Access, Achievement, and Wellness for Students of Color," https://sites.ed.gov/whieeaa/files/2016/10/Disrupting-Implicit-Bias-FINAL.pdf.

5. James T. Patterson, *Brown v. Board of Education: A Civil Rights Milestone and Its Troubled Legacy* (New York, NY: Oxford University Press, 2001).

6. W. J. Reese, The Origins of the American High School (New Haven, CT: Yale University Press, 1995); D. B. Tyack, *The One Best System: A History of American Urban Education* (Cambridge, MA: Harvard University Press, 1974).

7. M. Apple, "Away with All Teachers: The Cultural Politics of Home Schooling," in *Home Schooling in Full View*, ed. B. S. Cooper (Greenwich, CT: Information Age Publishing, 2005), 75–95.

8. D. A. Erickson, "Homeschooling and the Common School Nightmare," in *Home Schooling in Full View*, ed. B. S. Cooper (Greenwich, CT: Information Age Publishing, 2005), 21–44.

9. J. A. Avner, "Home Schoolers: A Forgotten Clientele?" *School Library Journal* 35, no. 11 (1989): 29–33, http://web.b.ebscohost.com.proxy.ulib.uits.iu.edu/ehost/pdfviewer/pdfviewer?sid=f8611841-a0f6-4ff9-94a8-75bf47c58894%40sessionmgr101&vid=6&hid=115.

10. P. Basham, J. Merrifield, and C. Hepburn, *Home Schooling: From the Extreme to the Mainstream* (Vancouver, BC, Canada: Fraser Institute, 2007); B. Ray, "A Homeschool Research Story," in *Home Schooling in Full View*, ed. B. S. Cooper (Greenwich, CT: Information Age Publishing, 2005), 1–19; B. Ray, "2.04 Million Homeschool Students in the United States in 2010," https://www.nheri.org/HomeschoolPopulationReport2010.pdf.

CHAPTER THREE

Homeschooling Today

Homeschooling and the COVID-19 Pandemic

Coronavirus disease 2019, abbreviated as COVID-19, has changed the way the world schools, lives, teaches, and learns. COVID-19 has created the most significant educational disruption in history. In May 2020, potentially at the peak of its ravages, COVID-19 had more than 90 percent of 1.5 billion youth globally learning from home. The United Nations Education, Scientific, and Cultural Organization's (UNESCO) Global Education Coalition began documenting and monitoring the school closures and affected learners in February 2020. Documentation and monitoring evolved over the time of COVID-19. At the UNESCO website (https://en.unesco.org/covid19/educationresponse), the user can watch school closures by country or area by date. The Global Education Coalition reports the statistics and percentages on its website, as well. The Global Education Coalition, founded by UNESCO, is an advocacy group for partnership and conversation to defend education throughout the unparalleled schooling interruption. More than 140 UN members worked together in civil society, academia, and the private sector to ensure that #LearningNeverStops.

The American (and global) nationwide school closures have been in response to an attempt to contain COVID-19. In a previous chapter, it was established that, while there is a US Department of Education, each state controls and manages education statewide. In early 2020, reports of the novel coronavirus began all over the world. By mid-February 2020, schools, left up

30 ~ Chapter Three

Figure 3.1. Saint John Catholic School Logan, Ohio, sign states "Ohio Mandated Closures." Dan Keck.

to the individual district's discretion, began to close for deep cleaning in New York and Washington State.

In January 2020, an article from *Education Week* titled "Coronavirus: How Some Schools Are Responding" states, "While federal health officials have said that the coronavirus is potentially a serious public health threat, most Americans, at this point, are not at risk. That, however, is not stopping educators from worrying and wondering how best to prepare for a possible case of coronavirus in their own schools and communities." During a February 4, 2020, press conference, the American Federation of Teachers President Randi Weingarten said, "Educators and school nurses need more specific instructions on what they should do to prepare for an increase in coronavirus cases in the United States."[1]

In late February 2020, the Centers for Disease Control and Prevention (CDC) issued a warning of potential COVID-19 surges that could interrupt daily life, including brick-and-mortar schooling institutions. "You should ask your children's schools about their plans for school dismissals or school closures," Nancy Messonnier, a director at the CDC, said during a press briefing. "Ask about plans for teleschool."[2]

Globally, schools began sending preventive notes home to families urging them to keep sick children home from school and to handwash frequently. Bothell High School was the first school to close in the US due to COVID-19. On February 27, 2020, it closed in Washington State for two days for deep cleaning after a school employee's relative tested positive for

Homeschooling Today ~ 31

Figure 3.2.   Day 41 remote school class meeting. Mario A. Pena.

COVID-19. By early March, schools began to announce building closures and transitioning to virtual schooling for 14 days. Two weeks turned into months as an unprecedented education disruption took place. Schooling, as we had known it before COVID-19, swiftly changed.

The transition to remote learning proved difficult for some families and worked effortlessly for others. The US Census Bureau conducted Household Pulse Surveys (HPS) for the pandemic's effect on American families in areas relating to employment, income, food and education. The HPS originated in joint effort via the US Census Bureau and seven federal agencies, in attempt respond to Americans during COVID-19 and garner data. The HPS also included a question about homeschooling, which relayed conclusive and crucial content; possibly the first data driven source at both the national and the state-level.

There has been a significant increase in home education as a result of COVID-19. Typically, when there is an event that affects education, there is an uptick in homeschooling. For example, after the Columbine shootings in 1999, some families became fearful and began schooling at home. According to the article "Columbine: Parents Bring Classrooms Home," Robin McDowell reports, "Educators in Colorado said there was a 30 percent to 40 percent increase in interest in homeschooling immediately after Dylan Klebold, 17, and Eric Harris, 18, went on their rampage April 20. The two seniors killed twelve classmates and a teacher and injured twenty-five others at Columbine High School before committing suicide."[3] The most recent data from the Department of Education shows the top three reasons parents choose to homeschool their children are dissatisfaction with academics, desire to provide moral instruction, and concern about school environments. Concern about school environments is at the top of 91 percent of parents' minds.[4]

The U.S. Census Bureau's experimental Household Pulse Surveys (HPS), give empirical insight on the impact of COVID-19 on homeschooling rates. Homeschooling numbers rose drastically across the country, and as of 2021 a record number of almost 20 percent of families chose to school from home. More families are seeking alternative educational options. The beginning of the 2020–2021 school year left many educational institutions with remote or virtual schooling, an unprecedented number of institutions with doors closed for in-person learning. The 2021–2022 school year offered majority of in person learning, with hotly debated masking and vaccination mandates. While pandemics are global, the nonpharmacological interventions (NPIs) are made by the state and local public health department based on the conditions in the area jurisdictions with "guidance from CDC (according to pandemic severity and potential efficacy) and governing authorities."[5] Individual states will use influenza surveillance indicators to help decide when to implement NPIs, such as school closures and other social distancing measures, in schools, workplaces, and public settings during a pandemic.[6]

To understand the impact of school closures and increase in homeschooling, let us explore the most recent pandemics of the 20th century. The article "Closure of Schools During an Influenza Pandemic," while a bit dated from 2009, is an excellent resource for further readings and historical context. The article defines school closure as an NPI that is often suggested for mitigating infection pandemics. The rationale for school closures is that the number of students in close contact would be decreased, thus not contributing to the virus's trajectories of exposures and spread. What is interesting about the study is that it references "social distancing," a term that has risen to mainstream jargon during the COVID-19 pandemic, stating that "recent reviews highlighted the lack of evidence for social distancing measures such as school closure. Even if benefits are substantial, they must be weighed against the potential high economic and social costs of proactively closing schools, which also can have negative effects on key workers since, for example, many doctors and nurses are also parents." In January 2006, the World Health Organization (WHO) published an article, "Nonpharmaceutical Interventions for Pandemic Influenza, National and Community Measures," that

Figure 3.3. A student learning at home due to COVID-19 school closures. Christina Giovannelli-Caputo.

referenced the 1957 Flu Pandemic[7] outbreaks that appeared in schools and army units. The conclusion was that avoiding the masses would reduce the viral spread.

Types of school closures, according to "Closure of Schools during an Influenza Pandemic,"[8] include the following:

- School closure: Closing of a school and sending of all the children and staff home
- Class dismissal: A school remains open with administrative staff, but most children stay home
- Reactive closure: Closure of a school when many children, staff, or both are experiencing illness
- Proactive closure: Closure of a school or class dismissal before substantial transmission among the school children

In 2017, the CDC came out with a study called "Get Your School Ready for Pandemic Flu," which offers guidelines for brick-and-mortar schools during a pandemic. It references many of the same NPIs—handwashing, social distancing, mask wearing, and school closures. The article says, "Plan ways to continue educating students if schools are temporarily dismissed. Consider using Web-based instruction, email, social media, local television, radio stations, or U.S. mail,"[9] setting the educational stage for us today.

The COVID-19 school closures and the "new-normal" life of "stay home, stay safe" have historical roots from the 14th century. The alternative mitigation strategies and interventions have a long history with pandemics. The exercise of quarantine began in the 14th century to protect seaside trade towns from sickness outbreak epidemics. According to the CDC website, "Ships arriving in Venice from infected ports were required to sit at anchor for forty days before landing. This practice, called quarantine, was derived from the Italian words *quaranta giorni*, which mean forty days."[10]

The CDC published an article in February 2007, "Local Mitigation Strategies for Pandemic Influenza," of pre-pandemic mitigation procedures that involved and recommended school closures as a vital social distancing strategy. "A recent study estimated that during the influenza season, nearly 75 percent of childhood influenza cases were infected by other children while in school, and 35 percent of all adult illnesses were thought to have been transmitted to them by school-age children."[11] School closures are thought to slow the spread of the virus and are used as an NPI.

The 1918 Flu Pandemic

Since the origin of life, there have been pandemics and plagues that have spread around the world. One of the most well-known in recent history is the

Influenza (Flu) Pandemic of 1918, also known as the "Spanish Flu." There were two waves of the 1918 flu, and the time frame was from 1918–1919. Among influenza developing in the US in the latter part of 1918, the American educational arrangement experienced a succession of powerful "physical, social, and pedagogical" changes.[12]

Many urban schools closed during the 1918 Flu Pandemic, some for as long as 15 weeks. According to the CDC website, around one-third of the world's population had contracted the deadly flu.

Three large cities did not close their school doors: Chicago, Illinois; New York City, New York; and New Haven, Connecticut. The absenteeism rates in Chicago during the 1918 Pandemic were high; they began at 30 percent in early October and rose to 50 percent by the end of October. These three cities granted parental choice on in-person learning. The three cities kept the schools open, stating the students were "better off in school," and the cleaning efforts were greatly magnified. These three cities regarded the open school buildings not as a relinquishment of public well-being accountability but as a chance to instrument the communal health policies of "school medical inspection and intensified disease surveillance."[13]

The 1937 Polio Epidemic

The 1937 Polio Epidemic seemed specifically to target children, which in turn triggered school closures. Schools in the Chicago area were closed for four weeks. While the youth were learning from home, the radio became an essential tool for facilitating learning. The remote learning model that is currently being used in today's schools was used back in 1937. Instead of schooling on computers (they were not invented yet), the youth of yesteryear had the radio.

Many indications for school closings came from past influenza experiences, for example, the 2009 H1N1 influenza pandemic in which youth were suspiciously affected. At the time, the US shut down about 700 schools, but the closures were locally related and for a short amount of time. The schools of the past served a slightly different purpose than in 2021. Today, there are many more schooling institutions, including daycare and nursery schools, that some youth attend for 12 hours a day while their parents work. Schooling has evolved and moved with the current times.

Some families rely on schools for food, shelter, safety, and childcare. The school closures associated with COVID-19 have affected vulnerable populations. Schools that have shut down in-person learning for an extended time frame could have negative social and health aftereffects for poverty-ridden

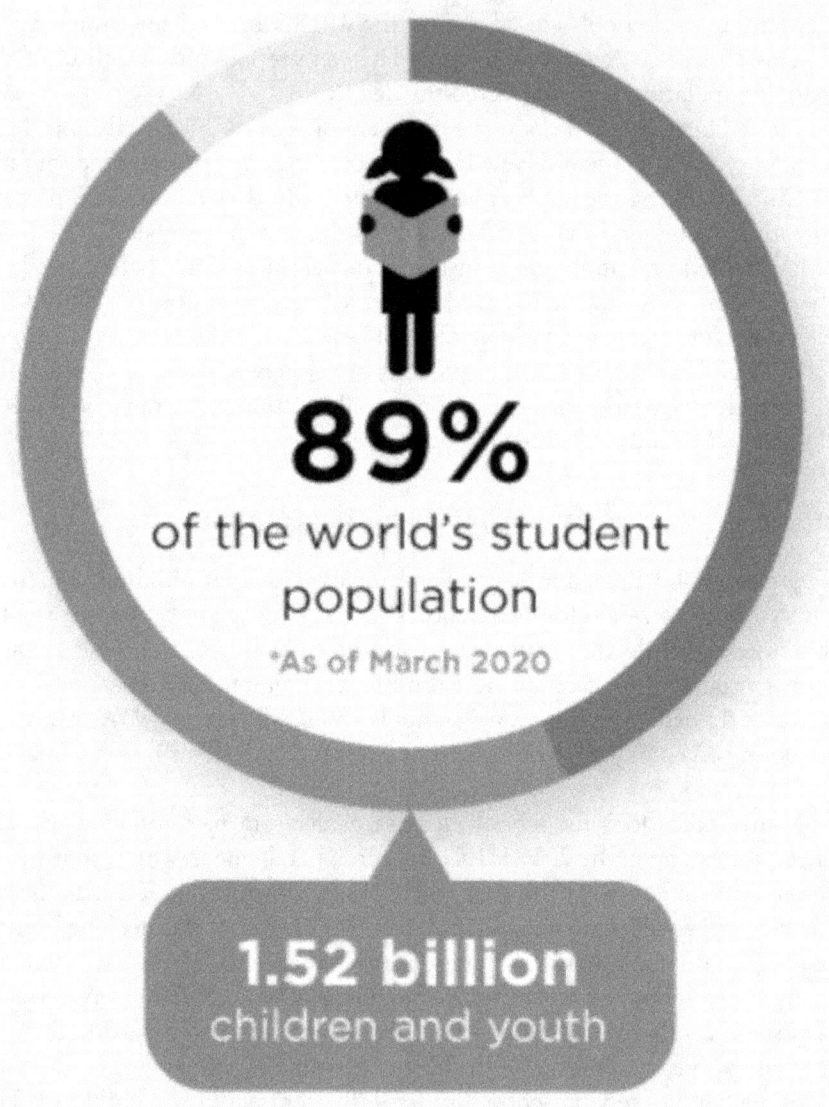

Figure 3.4. March 2020 Children and youth out of school due to COVID-19 closures. Photo Credit: by UN Women.

youth. The school closures, sadly, will potentially worsen current disparities. In education, there is the notion of the "Summer Slide," in which youth fall behind their grade level during the summer months when they are out of school. While the school closures and remote schooling are different from the summer closures, there will be an educational slide.

"It is imperative that we validate the experiences of the young during this global crisis, that we listen to their creative solutions for coping and connecting, and that we empower them to utilize their new skills to create a more robust, caring, and connected society as we emerge into the changed world," according to Lancelot Child Health.[14]

As a result, the learning gap has n widened in lower- to low-income families. Youth from lesser socioeconomic groups might live in conditions that made homeschooling and at-home learning difficult, that is, quiet workspaces, readiliy avail internet and devices. Just as there is no one size fits all approach to education methods, the pandemic schooling disruption did not fit all families. Remote and online learning typically necessitate expensive equipment and steady, reliable internet, both of which cost.

"In the USA, an estimated 2–5 percent of students in public schools do not live in a stable residence. The current health crisis could become a social crisis that will have long-lasting consequences for children in low-income families," according to A. M. Stern in "Better Off in School."[15]

In New York City, "where a large proportion of COVID-19 cases in the [US] have been observed, one in ten students were homeless or experienced severe housing instability during the previous school year."[16]

School closures also exacerbate food insecurity. In the US, 14 percent of youth were impacted by food insecurity in 2018.[17] Studies and research indicate that youth learn more effectively when they eat from a healthy, well-balanced diet. Academic achievements and food are closely tied. Schools across the nation attempted to combat food insecurity by offering free food pickup to all youth nationwide during school closures to ensure youth had access to food. US Department of Agriculture (USDA) Food and Nutrition Division worked with schools to provide youth who rely on free or reduced-price meals at school get the nutrition they need. In conjunction with USDA, Hunger Free America hosts a hotline for food resources to aid food insecurity across the US (1-866-3-HUNGRY or 1-877-8-HAMBRE [for Spanish]).

Students experienced an educational disruption of great magnitude that will imact generations to come. Libraries can help combat learning loss, with the educational pleathora of resources and subject experts.

Figure 3.5. U.S. Department of Agriculture (USDA) Food and Nutrition Service (FNS) National School Lunch Program (NSLP) Seamless Summer Option (SSO) alternative to traditional congregant feeding; this affords safe distancing with curbside distribution during the COVID-19 pandemic in the neighborhoods supported by the Harlandale Independent School District (HISD), in San Antonio, TX. USDA.

Research indicates homeschooling is on the rise across socioeconomic classes, religions, and cultures.[18] Legalities are a hot topic to the home educated, for not long ago, it was illegal to homeschool within the US. It was not until 1993 that it became legal in all 50 states, with Mississippi the final state to legalize home education. Home education's historical context is a complicated and challenging story to tell, as there is no one history. While there is a US Department of Education, individual American states control and depict education at the state level. Technically, there are fifty histories and stories of home education.

Home School Legal Defense Association (HSLDA)

https://hslda.org/

Librarians should not give legal advice to homeschooling patrons or customers. As employees of the library, librarians and staff must remain unbiased while offering resources. At the same time, librarians and staff must know where to point homeschooling customers when a legal question arises.

The Home School Legal Defense Association (HSLDA) is an Evangelical Christian homeschooling group and possibly the most encompassing legal protection for homeschoolers. Direct customer questions to the state level of where the library resides and to HSLDA.

The HSLDA was established in direct response to the growing homeschool community. As stated in chapter 2, two homeschooling attorney fathers, Mike Harris and Mike Smith, began HSLDA in 1983, which now serves as a major contender in homeschooling rights. The HSLDA.org website is inclusive and filled with in-depth information for the layperson and the homeschooling family. The mission of HSLDA is "To preserve and advance the fundamental, God-given, constitutional right of parents and others legally responsible for their children to direct their education."[19] When HSLDA was founded, only a handful of states allowed legal homeschooling.

In the late 1980s, when home education was growing and families were facing immense pressure to send their children to brick-and-mortar public schools, HSLDA offered legal representation with a yearly membership at the state and national levels.

Families can join the HSDLA for $130 a year per family. The membership fee includes legal protection, educational support, and strength in the community, according to HSLDA.org. The membership offers legal benefits and 24/7 on-call support. HSLDA and school choice advocates' laws gradually began to gain legal acceptance and recognition. While HSLDA has a strong focus on legalities, there is much more to the company than legal information. It is highly recommended that library professionals peruse the website to learn more for patron reference; you will use it when serving the homeschool community. HSLDA has a portion of its website dedicated to legalities by state, which is very user friendly.

HSLDA is a Christian site. For non-religious homeschooling resources, try the Homeschooling.com and A2Zhomeschooling.com.

- Homeschooling.com is also recommended for state legalities on education and homeschooling information. It is a secular site that is updated frequently.
- A2ZHomeschooling.com, an inclusive and in-depth site with lots of great content for new and seasoned homeschoolers. A2ZHomeschooling offers information by state and by region.

Board of Education (BOE) by State

Librarians must be aware of the homeschooling legalities in the state where their library resides. While a librarian should not offer legal advice, they are expected to know where to direct the customer and to be aware of the state's legalities. Each state has differing homeschooling laws and regulations, which have been set forth by each state's board of education (BOE). For example, I live in and serve the population in a suburb of Chicago, Illinois. The Illinois BOE website (https://www.isbe.net/Pages/Homeschool.aspx) is what I would print out/direct for a patron looking for more information. Librarians must know the content for the population the library serves.

For non-religious homeschooling resources, try the Homeschooling.com and A2Zhomeschooling.com:

- Homeschooling.com is also recommended for state legalities on education and homeschooling information. It is a secular site that is updated frequently.
- A2ZHomeschooling.com, an inclusive and in-depth site with lots of great content for new and seasoned homeschoolers. A2ZHomeschooling offers information by state and by region.

International Center for Home Education Research (ICHER)

https://www.icher.org/icher.html

International Center for Home Education Research (ICHER) was founded in 2012 by a group of scholars. ICHER is not a homeschooling advocacy group like HSLDA. There are three goals to ICHER, according to the website.

- "to provide nonpartisan information about homeschooling to media outlets and the public,
- to offer detailed analyses of emerging research on home education, and
- to encourage networking and collaboration among scholars."

The ICHER website has legal information, research, and enrollment data through 2018 and professional development globally.

Textbox 3.1
"Home education is currently illegal in Germany and essentially banned in Sweden. Parents in these countries frequently face hefty fines, court battles, jail time, and the removal of their children from the home—simply for their decision to teach them. In addition, a number of countries around the globe seek to severely limit parents' rights to make decisions about their children's education. These countries include Bulgaria, China, Cyprus, Greece, Macedonia, the Netherlands, Romania, and Spain. Even in countries where there is freedom to home educate, such as the United States, families must continue to fight to maintain the freedom to raise their children." —Global Home Education Exchange

Global Home Education Exchange (GHEX)

https://ghex.world/

Global Home Education Exchange (GHEX) is an international homeschooling advocacy group that hosts conferences and professional development. GHEX circles back to HSLDA and ICHER for legalities and online research. GHEX is a community for all supporters of school choice to get support, advice, and connect.

National Home Education Research Institute (NHERI)

https://www.nheri.org/

NHERI is a national leader on homeschool research and compiles the information on home education in the publication the Home School Researcher and on the website (NHERI.org). Dr. Brian Ray is a highly regarded researcher and one of the founders of NHERI, which originated in 1990. The website has expansive research and data collected for perusal. NHERI specializes in home education, research, data, facts, academic articles, and content. "More empirical evidence shows that homeschooling doubled in the United States during the government pandemic lockdowns. The growth occurred from the 2019–2020 institutional school year to the 2020–2021 year, to perhaps as many as 5 million school-age children. The latest data comes from the US Census Bureau, according to Dr. Brian Ray.

Coalition for Responsible Home Education (CRHE)

https://responsiblehomeschooling.org

Coalition for Responsible Home Education (CRHE) advocates and empowers home-educated youth by "educating the public and advocating for child-centered, evidence-based policy and practices for families and professionals," according to the website. The website goes on to share the vision of CRHE, which is, "Homeschooled children's right to a comprehensive and empowering education and a safe and supportive home environment is affirmed and protected by laws, stakeholders, and society as a whole."

CRHE was founded in 2013 by homeschooling advocates. The basic premise of the organization is a call to action for regulations surrounding home education. CRHE believes in a standard of rules and protection of the invisible children. There are homeschool families that are against CRHE and call it an anti-home-education group. CRHE believes and calls for documentation and annual notice (to the state BOE) for intent to school at home. Some homeschooling families believe that this infringes on their right of school choice, while CRHE believes it ensures the safety of abused/invisible children. It is important to note the differences in HSLDA and CRHE and be fluent in both resources.[20] "HSLDA and CRHE's positions on homeschooling policy differ because they serve two different audiences: HSLDA's mission is 'to defend and advance the constitutional right of *parents* to direct the education of their children' while CRHE's goal is 'advocating for homeschooled *children*,'" according to CRHE.

Tim Tebow

https://timtebow.com/

Tim Tebow paved the way for homeschoolers to participate in brick-and-mortar school athletics and extracurriculars. The question might arise while a librarian is on a service point, if a homeschooled student may play a sport through the local public school. The answer and regulations are dependent on the state level; just as the state BOE regulates schooling, the sports allotments are also regulated by the state. There is not a nationwide regulation on at-home learner students and sports.

The Tim Tebow bill is coined after the professional athlete who became the first home-educated player to be nominated for the Heisman Trophy. Tebow shed light and advocated for equality of access for homeschooled youth. Officially the bill is Equal Opportunity for Access in Education Act, and sports inclusion is only a small portion of the act. The bill does not provide students' equity of resources; it ensures that all students have access equity. Yet it is commonly referred to as the "Tim Tebow Law," and it gained public notoriety through his celebrity. The same goes for all extracurricular activities for the home-educated youth, all dependent by state level. At-home learners and homeschooled youth are eligible to participate in extra-curriculars per state approval.

Legalities

Today, all 50 states honor and respect the rights of parents to educate their children freely at home. In recent history, this was not always the case. While there has not been a case tried in the US Supreme Court regarding homeschooling, lawsuits and court cases have paved the way for the home educational rights that families know today. There have been precedents linking parental (or caregiver) school choice efforts with free speech and the free exercise of religion.

Pierce v. Society of Sisters 1925
Compulsory attendance laws were being adopted and instituted state by state in the early part of the twentieth century. In November 1922, Oregon School Bill, also known as Oregon Compulsory Attendance Act mandated all youth ages 8–16 attend a public school in the area in which they resided. The Society of the Sisters of the Holy Names of Jesus and Mary operated private Catholic schools in Oregon.

Catholic leaders feared that the KKK planned to push similar laws in other states, abolishing school choice. The Society of the Sisters , immediately took action. The Sisters filed a lawsuit in Oregon against the Governor Walter Pierce, States Attorney General Issaac Van Winkle, and District Attorney of Multnomah County Stanley Myers. The Hill Military Academy, a private school in Oregon, joined forces with the Sisters in filing a case. The cases were tried, heard, and decided together—and the judges granted an injunction in an Oregon District Court. The Sisters and Hill appealed their case to the US Supreme Court.

The Supreme Court ruled unanimously in favor of school choice—"the fundamental liberty upon which all governments in this Union repose excludes any general power of the State to standarize its children by forcing them to accept instruction from public teachers only."[21] The Supreme Court based the judgment on the due process clause of the Fourteenth Amendment, from which the Court decided, "The child is not the mere creature of the State; those who nurture him and direct his destiny have the right, coupled with the high duty, to recognize and prepare him for additional obligations."

For further reading: *Pierce v. Society of Sisters* - 268 U.S. 510

Wisconsin v. Yoder

Wisconsin v. Yoder (406 US 205) was argued in front of the Supreme Court in 1972. Three Amish teens in New Glarus, Green County, Wisconsin, from separate families—Frieda Yoder, age 15; Barbara Miller, age 15; and Vernon Yutzy, age 14—were withdrawn from public school after they finished their eighth-grade year. The compulsory education age in Wisconsin was 16, and youth were required to attend a schooling institution until then. A school administrator filed a complaint, and the Amish parents were fined $5. *Wisconsin v. Yoder* spoke on the constitutional equilibrium amid state power between Wisconsin compulsory education law and the rights of three members, Jonas Yoder, Wallace Miller, and Adin Yutzy, of the Old Order Amish religion and the Conservative Amish Mennonite Church.

The Supreme Court sided in favor of the Amish families' right to religious freedom and to educate their children in traditional Amish religious beliefs.[22]

Virtual Schooling

Before COVID-19, some states had instituted virtual schooling as a part of the public school curriculum. While the youth were learning a public curriculum, they were learning from home, and I define them as "at-home learners." Florida Virtual School (FLVS) (https://www.flvs.net/) instituted award-winning virtual schooling in 1997 for K–12. FLVS, the district, and its schools are accredited by Cognia (https://www.cognia.org/) and offer supportive online learning to students in Florida and worldwide. In March 2020, most schools in America shifted to the virtual model of learning. eLearning was transitioned to the teacher teaching via a remote or virtual platform and the youth learning from home. The unexpected global shift to remote learning and away from the brick-and-mortar classroom has many people wondering if eLearning will continue after COVID-19 and impact the future educational landscape.

Part-Time Attendance and the Homeschooled Student

Some families may choose part-time attendance. Each state is going to have different regulations and guidelines; refer to the home state for directives. This content was taken from the Illinois H.O.U.S.E. (http://www.illinoishouse.org/part-time-school-attendance), where I direct families for more information.

The law in Illinois explains the student must be accepted into any part of an academic course or program of the home public school where the youth is enrolled. The notice and application for partial attendance must be made by May 1 of the year before the desired enrollment. If there is sufficient space in the public school desired to be attended, the student can be accepted on a part-time basis. Participation in extracurricular programs for non-public school students is at the discretion of the school administration.

How can the library help? This question has been on the forefront of libraries since the beginning of the pandemic. The COVID-19 slide needs to be addressed, and the library is a community institution able to assist. Get to know the schooling community through servant leadership, community engagement, and outreach. During a pandemic, it can be challenging to create connections when we are all scared. We must keep staff and patrons safe by allowing for what the community needs with safety interventions in place. A simple phone call, an email, or a virtual visit can start conversations. Unless we try, we do not know what will spark a relationship.

As librarians and library staff who work at a public service desk, it is imperative to serve the public by answering their reference needs. Be aware of the educational community the library serves. Know the schooling options, the state regulations, and the community's strengths while learning what the deficits are. The community will grow from the library's advocacy in the educational arena.

Notes

1. A. Prothero, "Teachers' Union Gives Guidance for Schools on Coronavirus," Education Week, February 11, 2020, https://www.edweek.org/ew/articles/2020/02/12/teachers-union-gives-guidance-for-schools-on.html.

2. Mark Lieberman, "Schools Should Prepare for Coronavirus Outbreaks, CDC Officials Warn," Education Week, February 25, 2020, https://www.edweek.org/leadership/schools-should-prepare-for-coronavirus-outbreaks-cdc-officials-warn/2020/02.

3. Robin McDowell, "Columbine: Parents Bring Classrooms Home," Kitsap Sun, July 7, 1999, https://products.kitsapsun.com/archive/1999/07-07/0080_columbine__parents_bring_classroo.html.

4. R. Hanson and C. Pugliese, "Parent and Family Involvement in Education: 2019," Washington, DC: National Center for Education Statistics, 2020, https://nces.ed.gov/pubs2020/2020076full.pdf.

5. N. Qualls et al., "Community Mitigation Guidelines to Prevent Pandemic Influenza—United States, 2017," *Morbidity and Mortality Weekly Report* 66, no. 1 (2017): 1–34, https://www.cdc.gov/mmwr/volumes/66/rr/pdfs/rr6601.pdf.

6. Ibid.

7. Centers for Disease Control and Prevention, "Nonpharmaceutical Interventions for Pandemic Influenza, National and Community Measures," *Emerging*

Infectious Diseases 12, no. 1 (2006): 88–94, https://wwwnc.cdc.gov/eid/article/12/1/05-1371_article.

8. Simon Cauchemez, Neil M. Ferguson, Claude Wachtel, Anders Tegnell, Guillaume Saour, Ben Duncan, and Angus Nicoll, "Closure of Schools during an Influenza Pandemic," *The Lancet Infectious Diseases* 9, no. 8 (2009): 473–81.

9. Centers for Disease Control and Prevention, "Get Your Community Ready for Pandemic Influenza, 2017," April 2017, https://www.cdc.gov/nonpharmaceutical-interventions/pdf/gr-pan-flu-npi.pdf.

10. Centers for Disease Control and Prevention, "History of Quarantine," accessed June 18, 2021, https://www.cdc.gov/quarantine/historyquarantine.html.

11. Robert J. Glass, Laura M. Glass, and Walter E. Beyeler, "Local Mitigation Strategies for Pandemic Influenza," National Infrastructure Simulation & Analysis Center, December 2005, https://www.sandia.gov/CasosEngineering/_assets/documents/NISAC_FluMitigationPaperWithFullSOMTables_12_21_05.pdf.

12. A. M. Stern et al., "'Better Off in School': School Medical Inspection as a Public Health Strategy during the 1918–1919 Influenza Pandemic in the United States," *Public Health Reports* 125, no. 3 (1974): 63–70, https://doi.org/10.1177/00333549101250S309.

13. Ibid.

14. "Pandemic School Closures: Risks and Opportunities," *The Lancet Child & Adolescent Health* 4, no. 5 (2020): 341. https://doi.org/10.1016/S2352-4642(20)30105-X.

15. Stern, "'Better Off in School.'"

16. W. Van Lancker and Z. Parolin, "COVID-19, School Closures, and Child Poverty: A Social Crisis in the Making," *The Lancet Public Health* 5, no 5 (2020): e243–44, https://doi.org/10.1016/S2468-2667(20)30084-0.

17. US Department of Agriculture, "Food Security in the United States," updated September 9, 2020, https://www.ers.usda.gov/data-products/food-security-in-the-united-states/.

18. Brian Ray, "Homeschooling Growing: Multiple Data Points Show Increase 2012 to 2016 and Later," National Home Education Research Institute, http://www.nheri.org/homeschool-population-size-growing/.

19. Homeschool Legal Defense Association, "Our Mission," https://hslda.org/post/our-mission#:~:text=In%20short%2C%20our%20mission%20is%20to%20make%20homeschooling%20possible.&text=For%20over%2035%20years%2C%20HSLDA,long%20as%20we're%20around.

20. Collation for Responsible Homeschooling, "Why Homeschooling Needs Oversight: Responding to HSLDA and WORLD," https://responsiblehomeschooling.org/why-homeschooling-needs-oversight-responding-to-hslda-and-world/#:~:text=HSLDA%20and%20CRHE's%20positions%20on,.%E2%80%9D%20In%20theory%2C%20though%2C.

21. Pierce v. Society of Sisters (1925). Oyez. Retrieved March 23, 2021, from https://www.oyez.org/cases/1900-1940/268us510.

22. Wisconsin v. Yoder (1972), First Amendment Encyclopedia, accessed March 12, 2021, https://mtsu.edu/first-amendment/article/676/wisconsin-v-yoder.

CHAPTER 4

Different Homeschooling Methods

One of the missions of a public library is to support the community, including local schools. Before COVID-19, the estimated national average of homeschoolers, according to the National Center for Educational Statistics (NCES), was 3.5 percent of school-aged youth.[1] There are no hard and fast numbers documented of the number of home-educated youth. All are estimated percentages that have been documented in various surveys; the most notable is NCES. The Household Pulse Surveys (HPS) documented the homeschool growth during COVID-19 with numbers climbing, 5.4 percent in the spring of 2020, 11.1 percent in the fall of 2020, and 19.5 percent in the spring of 2021. The board of directors, trustees at the library, and library administration may ask for data, refer to NCES and HPS, as well as the local homeschooling groups.

Get to know the community the library serves. The following chapters will give real-life examples of how to build and foster these relationships. Compile data about the library and community after the library is involved with the home educated. For example, while the national estimated average is around 3.5 percent, upon learning about the homeschooled youth local to my library, I could estimate before COVID-19 the local home-educated school-aged youth percentage was 6 percent. That is 2.5 percent higher than the national estimated average. These numbers and research can be used as a platform for building library services.

There are home-educated youths in all the areas the library serves. It is imperative to make connections and provide resources. The NCES Parent and Family Involvement Survey (PFI) cites the library as one of the most used resources by homeschooled families.² Seventy-eight percent of home-educated families use the public library, citing the public library as their biggest and best resource. In short, at-home learner families love librarians.

Alternative Education Methods (AEMs)

AEMs and *schooling diversity* are terms I developed and coined to describe the other schooling methods families in our communities employ. Most people in the nation have attended or graduated from public schooling; however, there is a growing trend of alternative methods. COVID-19 exasperated schooling techniques by placing over 90 percent of all youth globally as at-home learners.³ At-home learners, remote, and homeschool, are educational methodologies that overlap and are not exclusive in their meaning. Formal and informal education are concepts that intersect as well. All schooling was once done outside of a building's walls, as there were no brick-and-mortar institutions. There are infinite ways of schooling, and there is no one size fits all approach to education. Children are unique individuals, each one as different as a fingerprint. No two fingerprints are identical, and no two youth have the same fingerprints. While some fingerprints may be similar, they are not 100 percent identical. The same goes for learning styles. Some people may and will have similar learning styles, but they will not all learn in the same way. Schooling is personal; the way families choose to educate and raise their families is personal. As John Taylor Gatto said in his book *Dumbing Us Down*, "Whatever an education is, it should make you a unique individual, not a conformist; it should furnish you with an original spirit to tackle the big challenges; it should allow you to find values which will be your road map through life; it should make you spiritually rich, a person who loves whatever you are doing, wherever you are, whoever you are with; it should teach you what is important, how to live and how to die."

Pandemic schooling has proven difficult for some families, my family included. The school closures came when my children's educational journey (pre-K, kindergarten, and first grade) was essential to their growth. On March 13, 2020, my children came home from school and did not return. Remote schooling fell onto my husband's and my shoulders. The COVID-19 one size fits all eLearning option from the local school did not work for us. The teachers, beloved by my children, were resiliently rushing to learn a new model of education. One child struggling with ADHD could not sit still during a virtual lesson, our preschooler needed to play, and the first grader was rapidly becoming addicted to the screen, all while we welcomed our fourth child in March of 2020. As the world was shutting down and future of education was unknown, I saw the light go out of my children's eyes at the mention of school.

Our family stopped forcing ourselves to learn in a way that was harmful to our children. With my knowledge of home education and AEMs, I shared what I knew with other families, promoting the library and the school library

Figure 4.1. Three Caputo kids homeschooling during COVID-19. Christina Giovannelli-Caputo.

Figure 4.2. Three Caputo kids homeschooling during COVID-19. Christina Giovannelli-Caputo.

Figure 4.3. Three Caputo kids homeschooling during COVID-19. Christina Giovannelli-Caputo.

for support. My children began attending Wild+Free, an outdoor free play with local homeschoolers. As COVID-19 raged on, I became more vocal on our family's educational plan. We were featured in a *74 Million* article, "As Distance Learning Pushes Parents into Pods, Some Look for Ways to Make the Model More Inclusive."[4] We adjusted, played, explored, wandered, and read. We read *a lot*! I read book after book on at-home learning methods. As a former classroom teacher, I was surprised to learn that my view on home education aligned with Holt's and Gatto's radical philosophies, validating the need for differentiation of methods.

Curricula

One of the most common homeschool reference questions is on curricula. Curricula for homeschooling is as varied and diverse as the methods. I often refer families to a website, "Cathy Duffy Homeschool Reviews," at https://cathyduffyreviews.com. Duffy has been reviewing homeschool curricula since 1994; the website is in depth and offers advanced searching. Duffy is the author of several books on the topic of homeschool curricula. Some libraries circulate curricula with extended due dates. The Homeschool Resource Center (HRC) at the Johnsburg Public Library in Johnsburg, Illinois, is the biggest and most famous source of homeschool curricula in the Midwest. All items from the HRC can be checked out for six weeks and may be renewed online or via phone for an additional six weeks. The HRC offers a "try it before you buy it" approach to homeschool curricula. Kathy Wentz, from the HRC, believes that homeschool families change philosophies and curricula seven times in the first two years. She offers support to the homeschooling community through her passion for AEMs. Wentz can be contracted to present programs at libraries nationally on offering and growing services to homeschool services. She can be contacted via her website, Wentz Educational Services at https://kathywentz.blogspot.com/.

Compulsory education is a new phenomenon in the grand scheme of things. Home education has historically been the baseline of schooling since the beginning of time. All the homeschooling techniques and methods go hand in hand. They can all be interwoven and used simultaneously. It is the beauty of home education; it is modeled and explicitly molded to each family and youth. Eclectic homeschooling is an AEM where caregivers select portions of several different philosophies and curriculums. Eclectic homeschooling is a popular flexible method, where parents can design a schedule and curriculum unique to each student.

Learning in a Classroom	Learning in a Homeschool
• Learning takes place at defined times • Teachers must design instruction that is aimed at the "average" student • Most instruction takes place in the classroom environment • Students must contend with many distractions, and teachers must contend with many interruptions • Curriculum is decided at the state and regional level • Each subject covered is allotted a specific frame of instructional time • Standardized testing and frequent assessments are the norms for evaluating student achievement • Students are usually required to sit and observe quietly to preserve a conducive learning environment for all students • Grading scales are applied to help teachers evaluate student progress and make comparisons between students	• Learning can happen any time of day or night • Instruction can be customized to each individual student • Homeschoolers have the flexibility to learn anywhere: at home, in the car, in the outdoors, and on frequent field trips • The homeschool environment can offer a 1:1 teaching/learning ratio with few distractions and interruptions • Parents and students usually can choose their curricula and resources • The time dedicated to each subject covered can be determined individually, and acceleration or remediation can be applied as needed • Parents are working so closely with their homeschooler that they can often track achievement without frequent testing • Students are free to learn in whatever mode suits them best, even if that means moving around, frequent breaks, and incorporating a hands-on practice • Grading scales may or may not be necessary depending on parent/student needs

Figure 4.4. Time4Learning Chart. The following chart from Time4Learning shares differences between classroom instruction and learning in a homeschool setting. [i]. Time4Learning.

Deschooling

Deschooling is thought of as a transition period from traditional brick-and-mortar school to homeschool with little to no formal schoolwork. The thought is to reset the youth's natural and intuitive love of learning. During this time, the parents will observe their child while letting the child explore. Brick-and-mortar schools, both public and private, educate a classroom full of students at a time. Home education may have multiple children involved per family or group, yet, typically, it is more of an individualized approach.

The caregivers can use the deschooling period to recognize how the youth learns and how the home experience will be different than a traditional classroom.

There are differences between classroom and homeschooling settings, and the child and parent will need time to adjust. There are no set time frames for the deschooling transition to be completed; it all depends on the youth and family. The common thought is that, the longer the child was in a traditional schooling setting, the longer the deschooling process might take. During this time, families take field trips, incorporate unit studies, play, hike, travel, and do whatever is comfortable. Some families may use Kahn Academy, Outschool, and Time4Learning during the deschooling process. While others may not use any sort of structured learning. It all depends on the family and child. For further reading on Deschooling from a parents perspective, read The Truth about Deschooling that Will Blow Your Mind at Educatedadventures.com (https://educatedadventures.com/2016/03/16/the-truth-about-deschooling-that-will-blow-your-mind/?fbclid=IwAR0wIYWJO1dJ6ZKTYrBsUYkgHwrTuVBVqTbGmv5LGJ48jxqAV7EAI21DFW8).

The library can offer support for families deschooling and transitioning AEMs by offering programming during a traditional school day and weekly meetups. It is recommended to know the deschooling process, as patrons may ask the librarian what is involved. I also recommend knowing the different types of AEMs that families in the community might be utilizing. There are as many types and styles of AEMs as there are schools. There is no one size fits all approach to home education, and the methods will vary from family to family. It is best to engage with the community where your library serves to establish connections and learn more. Each family and community are unique. The following are popular AEMs used in homeschooling. The following is not a complete and comprehensive list or the only AEMs used in your communities, merely a place to start.

Traditional Homeschooling

Traditional home education is perhaps what you think of when you think of homeschooling. It is re-creating school at home using a set curriculum, and the caregiver is the primary instructor. This method may involve youth learning at home in a traditional way, and it may include other methods as well. Typically, the curriculum used is prepackaged and sold at grade levels. Dr. and Mrs. Moore, the grandparents of homeschooling, say on their website, the Moore Formula, "Hand in hand with homeschooling parents providing:

- individualized curriculum
- educational materials
- unit studies
- aid in learning disabilities
- gifted education assistance."

Marguerite, from St. Charles, Illinois, chose to homeschool grades four through seven for her daughter, who was involved in competitive figure skating, because it fits their schedule. Homeschool came full circle back to their family. She states, "We chose to homeschool for our son once he reached sixth grade. The decision was made due to extreme bullying in the public school. We told him we'd homeschool for a year and see what happened. He loved it so much (!) he chose to remain homeschooled through high school. Both of our children entered college as high honor students and maintained the skills of excellent time management and independent study." For this family, the curriculum used was Abeka (https://www.abeka.com/). They were not involved in a co-op due to timing in their schedule; however, they had an active social life with hockey and figure skating. Marguerite and her family are "huge advocates" of the public library and utilized many programs and classes while accrediting the library as an excellent home education resource.

I suggest learning about which AEMs are popular in the community where you serve. Popular education tools and resources for the traditional AEM for potential patron reference are Abeka, Easy Peasy All-in-One Homeschool, Kahn Academy, and Time4Learning.

Classical Homeschooling

The classical method of homeschooling involves the three learning stages—grammar, logic, and rhetoric. The grammar stage encompasses learned memorization, fact gathering, and knowledge connections. The logic stage is applying logic and reasoning to learning. The final of the trivium is rhetoric, which is when a student learns wisdom and judgment. A *Well-Trained Mind, Guide to a Classical Education at Home* by Susan Bauer and Jessie Wise is an example of a popular book on the method. The classical model typically uses real books, autobiographies, and primary sources as the textbooks. Classical Conversations is a widespread Christian homeschooling group that focuses on the classical method; more information can be found at ClassicalConversations.com. Popular educational tools and resources for the classical AEM for potential patron reference are Classical Conversations, Kolbe Academy, Veritas Press, and Well-Trained Mind.

> **Sidebar 4.1**
> Rachel, a homeschool mom of four from Chicago, shares, "For me, libraries are such a valuable resource. They supplement our learning and curriculum in so many ways. I would want librarians to know that we value them. We love infusing good books into our school day. We have the flexibility to spend more time reading, so we love great recommendations. For instance, if we are covering something about a historical period, we appreciate biographies, related historical fiction, etc.; displays in libraries that highlight quality books with a theme are great. For instance, we were recently studying the water cycle. Our library had a theme in its display featuring books on rain. It was great because I had a bunch of books related to our studies. You cannot predict what homeschool families are studying, but we do love books on various topics. Well-illustrated, mythological books, children's books with great storylines and characters appeal to us. We are always working with developing readers at different levels. So I love when librarians have suggested books for different reading levels. Recently, one of our librarians asked my son what he was interested in reading about, and then she took us row by row to suggest a few series about mythology. That gave us several options. I appreciated that."

Microschooling

Microschools differ in size, method, and authority, and these schools "model a combination of a one-room schoolhouse, blended learning, homeschooling, and private schooling."[5]

Microschools, or pods, have been reimagining the educational model; they are small educational programs. Microschools are small, tuition-based schools free from standardized tests and mandated curriculum and offer the flexibility and personalization of learning. Microschools have become known during the COVID-19 era as learning pods or pods, where a group of youths learn together through a hired tutor or AEM. During COVID-19, the eruption in pods is for some because of peer socialization. The group would remain cloistered among themselves, hence slowing the spread of coronavirus. There is no need for accreditation; that is a misconstrued fact that private schools need to have one. Some wonder if this method will increase learning disparities between classes and races, as it can be tuition based. There is no rule that microschools need to charge tuition; however, families may choose them that cannot afford private school tuition. Microschools and pods have the freedom to create schedules that work for the family, enroll youth of all age and grade levels, and allow for flexibility in hands-on learning.

Travel Schooling

Some families have chosen to go to school on the road. The schooling may be from a recreational vehicle while driving across the country, or it may be longer trips to various destinations. It can be everything or anything that the family needs. This method is newer to libraries, which involves traveling as a form of schooling. For example, a family may be learning about the colonial times and travel to Colonial Williamsburg (https://www.colonialwilliamsburg.org) to immerse themselves in the time. While learning about the Renaissance art period, they may travel to Italy to explore the Sistine Chapel. Schooling may be on the road with a parent who travels for work. I met a family that travel schools while living on a boat in the Caribbean. Travel schoolers often utilize the databases, eBooks, and online content the library offers. These families might be living in smaller quarters, so the virtual content is accessible and welcoming. Some indicators show that travel schooling is on the upswing. Some families have more flexibility during COVID-19, which has allowed work-from-home options for some companies. Travel schooling may employ various AEM curricula, eclectic homeschooling, or virtual schooling.

Sidebar 4.2
Mandy, a travel schooling parent, says, "We started homeschooling when we moved into an RV and got on the road. Our initial thought was to travel for one to five years. The impetus was my husband getting a remote job. We go to the local library each week. It is usually free reading time and playtime (I hated all the toys at our local library, and now I love them because we don't have to carry them around!). We sometimes plan to hit an event like story time or a STEM workshop, depending on timing. I have my library card from home and use it to borrow ebooks and audiobooks. We often pick up new-to-us books at Friends of Library book sale shelves."

Samantha, a travel schooling parent, shared, "We travel, so we decided to school while traveling. We use the library for most things needed (books and online). We are mostly internet and phone service free, so the library provides opportunities to research, download books, talk with locals, and participate in activities and a place to hang."

Unschooling

Unschooling is child-led learning. The parents or caregivers serve as the guide or facilitators, not necessarily the teachers. The child follows his or her interest in learning and does not follow a set curriculum. Patrick Farenga, a homeschooling self-directed learning advocate, says, "I broadly define unschooling as allowing your children as much freedom to explore the world around them in their own ways as you can comfortably bear; I see unschooling in the light of partnership, not in the light of the dominance of a child's wishes over a parents' or vice versa." Farenga worked closely with John Holt, the founder of coining the term "unschooling." Farenga writes and operates the John Holt/Growing Without Schooling website at www.johnholtgws.com. He is also a founding member of Alternatives to School at www.alternativestoschool.com. Popular educational tools and resources for the Unschooling AEM for potential patron reference are John Holt, Natural Child Project, Radical Unschooling, and School is Dead.

A popular unschoolers YouTube channel is "Karla and the Sensational Six." The link can be found in the endnote.[6] Karla Williams is a learning advocate, motivational speaker, home educator, and mom to six children. She is the author of the popular book *Homeschool Gone Wild*. Karla describes the YouTube channel as follows, "We are a family that is passionate about learning and growing together. We are unschoolers of six brilliant and motivated learners. We will be sharing what life looks like in our very active home as each of our six children take six separate roads to discover, explore, and enjoy the process of learning naturally!" Each day the family has a specific theme, such as "What in the World Tuesday" and "Read about It Wednesdays." The children learn through interest-led adventures. Williams says on educating her six children from home, "To enjoy the journey, love what they do, and make a difference in this world."

Unit Studies

Unit studies allow for a great deal of choice when homeschooling. This method often serves as a transition from deschooling to a form of homeschooling. Unit studies can be flexible or structured depending on the child's need. It is an in-depth study of a specific topic, allowing for the student's immersion, with all subjects youth led and taught around a topic. For example, if a child is interested in dinosaurs, all subjects would be taught around dinosaurs. Unit studies are an inexpensive model that can use resources from the internet and library. Popular educational tools and resources for the unit study AEM for potential patron reference are Amanda Bennett's Unit Study Adventures, Design-A-Study, Five in a Row, and KONOS.

Nature Schooling

Forest schools are growing in popularity in the US. Nature-led forest schools are holistically stimulated, play based, and child centered. Forest schooling originated from the Scandinavian *friluftsliv* culture (pronounced free-looffs-liv), which translates to "open-air living." This AEM has made its way to the US; families are noticing the outdoor research indicating benefits.[7] Families embrace noncognitive and social-emotional learning through nature schooling, which, for some, is taking precedence over demanding testing and state-level academics. Both the Forest School Foundation (https://www.theforestschoolfoundation.org/) and Natural Start Alliance (https://naturalstart.org/) have missions to support nature-based schooling options in the US.

A popular book, *The Call of the Wild and Free: Reclaiming Wonder in Your Child's Education* by Ainsley Arment, is a companion book to the homeschooling group Wild+Free (https://www.bewildandfree.org/). Wild+Free is a homeschooling group that originated from Arment's family's journey in home education. Arment writes in her book, "Our kids will have many opportunities for careers, discipline, and hard work. But they only get one childhood. So, let's make it magical." Arment was moved by Henry David Thoreau's saying, "All good things are wild and free," and started Wild+Free—"a community of mothers and families who want their children to receive a quality education at home, while also nurturing a sense of curiosity, joy, and awe that encompasses a positive childhood."[8] She gained a following on Instagram (https://www.instagram.com/ainsl3y/?hl=en), which in turn started a movement. Arment writes in her book that childhood has been lost to video games, sports leagues, and mobile devices, and society has forced children to have busy schedules just like their parents. A 2014 study by the American Psychological Association revealed that the average reported stress in school-aged youth during the school year exceeds that of adults.[9] Arment said, "For as long as humans have lived on this earth, children have been schooled at home. Still, we homeschooling mamas often feel like pioneers forging a new path for the next generation."

Some of these nature initiatives have been led by families concerned with the level of screen time that youth are encountering. "1000 Hours Outside" (https://www.1000hoursoutside.com/) has a mission to match outdoor time with screen time. The American Academy of Child and Adolescent Psychiatry (www.aacap.org) reported in February 2020 that the typical American

8- to 12-year-old youth spent four to six hours a day and teens nine hours a day on screens. The pandemic virtual and remote schooling options and social distancing mitigations have increased screen time dramatically since 2020. This has concerned some families, which has increased the interest in home-based education. Popular educational tools and resources for nature-based AEM for potential patron reference are Nature School, Samara Early Learning, Wild+Free, and Wilderchild.

Additional Methods

Steiner Education, more commonly known as the Waldorf Method, is a non-Christian but spiritual-based program that delays formal schooling with the arts and literature. The Waldorf Method's purpose is to educate the whole child—head, heart, and hands. More information can be found at https://www.waldorfeducation.org/waldorf-education.

Another common homeschooling method is the Montessori model. The adult is the guide, and the child is free to explore and learn through his or her free choices. The adult will provide teachable moments through brief lessons, with the concept of a structured environment conducive to child-led learning. More information can be found at https://amshq.org/Families/Why-Choose-Montessori.

Charlotte Mason (CM) is a Christian-based education model focusing on structure through strong literature, copying of material, and dictation. This model does not use textbooks and emphasizes daily nature experiences. The CM method uses living books, which make the written content come alive for the youth. Charlotte Mason can overlap with other AEM, often classical, unit studies,

Arment, Ainsley. *Call of the Wild and Free.*

Bogart, Judy. *The Brave Learner.*

Cohen, Cafi. *Homeschooling the Teen Years.*

Erickson, Jamie. *Homeschool Bravely.*

Gatto, John Taylor. *Dumbing Us Down.*

Gray, Peter. *Unschooled.*

Hewitt, Ben. *Home Grow.*

Holt, John. *How Children Learn.*

Mackenzie, Sarah. *Teaching from Rest.*

Penn-Nabrit, Paula. *Morning by Morning.*

Taylor, Dr. Myiesha. *The Homeschooling Alternative.*

Williams, Karla Marie. *Homeschool Gone Wild.*

Williams, Karla Maria. *Teens Unleashed.*

Figure 4.5. Recommended Reading on Homeschooling. Christina Giovannelli-Caputo.

and unschooling. More information can be found at https://simplycharlotte mason.com/.

I encourage you to create booklists or resource lists of the library's items for all homeschooling and at-home learning AEMs. Creating and having accessible resources will be greatly appreciated by the homeschooling and at-home learning community. Another helpful idea is an audit of the collection on homeschooling and at-home learning items. While you are at it, you might as well audit for the diversity of materials.[10]

Notes

1. National Center for Education Statistics, "Number and Percentage of Homeschooled Students Ages 5 through 17 with a Grade Equivalent of Kindergarten through 12th Grade, By Selected Child, Parent, and Household Characteristics: Selected Years, 1999 through 2016," https://nces.ed.gov/programs/digest/d19/tables/dt19_206.10.asp.

2. R. Hanson and C. Pugliese, "Parent and Family Involvement in Education: 2019," https://nces.ed.gov/pubs2020/2020076full.pdf.

3. "At-home learners" is a term coined and developed by the author as a direct result of COVID-19.

4. L. Jacobson, "As Distance Learning Pushes Parents into Pods, Some Look for Ways to Make the Model More Inclusive," *The 74 Million*, August 10, 2020, accessed March 28, 2021, https://www.the74million.org/article/as-distance-learning-pushes-parents-into-pods-some-look-for-ways-to-make-the-model-more-inclusive/.

5. M. B. Horn, "The Rise of AltSchool and Other Micro-Schools," *Education Next* 15, no. 3 (2015), https://www.educationnext.org/rise-micro-schools/.

6. "Karla and the Sensational Six," YouTube, https://www.youtube.com/channel/UCgYl2Rbg4kEx4AYDA8GJ3fg.

7. Forest School Foundation, "Supporting Research and Resources," https://www.theforestschoolfoundation.org/research-resources.

8. A. Arment. "Reclaiming Wonder in Your Childs Education," https://www.bewildandfree.org/book.

9. American Psychological Association, "American Psychological Association Survey Shows Teen Stress Rivals That of Adults" [Press release], February 11, 2014, http://www.apa.org/news/press/releases/2014/02/teen-stress.

10. K. Jensen, "Doing a YA Collection Diversity Audit: Resources and Sources (Part 3), November 2017, accessed March 31, 2021, https://www.teenlibrariantoolbox.com/2017/11/doing-a-diversity-audit-resources-and-sources-part-3/.

CHAPTER FIVE

The Public Library and Homeschoolers

Every Child Ready to Read (ECRR) at your library is a parent learning initiative that your library may support and use. Youth librarians across the country are familiar with ECRR (http://everychildreadytoread.org/), which was written and published by the Public Library Association (PLA) and Association of Library Services to Children (ALSC). ECRR supports the parents' notion and philosophy as the child's first teacher and is a parent and caregiver education initiative. It is a research-based ideology that recognizes the parents' and caregiver's impact on a child's early literacy. The program curriculum, developed in 2004, focuses on educating the parents and caregivers on the importance of early literacy and fostering school readiness in the home. The objective is that the public library's efforts can be replicated and multiplied, cultivating deeper early learning and growth. "The ECRR second edition toolkit resources enable public libraries and other early literacy centers to present workshops that help *prepare parents/caregivers for their critical role as their child's first teacher*. The workshops demonstrate how parents, grandparents, childcare providers, and preschool teachers can use five simple research-based practices—talking, singing, reading, writing, and playing—to develop language and pre-reading skills in children from birth to age five," according to the ECRR website.

The ECRR toolkit can be purchased from everychildreadytoread.org. Public librarians support the notion that the parent is a child's first teacher. Through this concept, the library supports the at-home learning community. The parent and caregiver are the child's first teachers, which has a long-standing history. Many of the ECRR tips can be shared and are shared in story times around the country. Libraries support the concept of the parent as the first teacher by offering services to families.

One of the American Library Association's (ALA's) fundamental ideologies is equity for all, with a mission and vision to support equity and inclusion through a lens of social justice to underserved populations. While cultural diversity is often thought of, school diversity is real in the communities we serve. School diversity is growing, while the achievement gaps from COVID-19 are also growing. Diversity of race, religion, creed, and socioeconomic class is present in all communities. The US Department of Education estimates that nearly 41 percent of all homeschooled youth (before COVID-19) are non-White. Homeschool education spans all demographics and is quickly growing in marginalized communities. School diversity includes cultural and racial differences in a set classroom and *schooling diversity*—alternative educational methodologies (AEMs).

The ALA Bill of Rights supports democracy and home education through diversity of materials and intellectual freedom in library services. The library is an extension of educational resources that is one of the sole places where patrons can access the information without cost. Libraries are essential to the communities to foster social progress through free access to information. Schooling diversity has grown in methods and within marginalized communities. Libraries and library staff must hold equity, diversity, and inclusion to the highest standard to meet all needs. The library is in a unique position to be of service to all patrons and residents.

Holly Eberle from Algonquin Area Public Library created a "Homeschool for Newcomers" video to deliver supportive services to homeschoolers and potential homeschoolers. The video was well received with many views. Many of the reference questions in August 2020 were on nonpublic school options in Algonquin.

Librarians and libraries serve *all*, regardless of schooling choice, background, culture, gender, and race. The youth of tomorrow are precious and valuable, and they all deserve to have the rich resources available to them by the library. Meaningful library service to youth is beneficial to the community when librarians and library staff have a wide range of skills and experiences. ALSC and Young Adult Library Services Association (YALSA) core competencies have solid groundings in serving our communities' diversity. The competencies offer a baseline for providing services while fostering connections and advocating for services.

Sidebar 5.1

Algonquin, Illinois, does have a lot of homeschool families that end up being "power users" of the library. I have gotten to know more about the homeschooling movement through them. At least three groups used our meeting rooms for co-op learning space in the past few years. We have a Homework Center collection, primarily workbooks that patrons may copy or use transparency sheets and dry erase markers to fill out. It isn't geared toward homeschool learners specifically, but neither are our STEM kits. I presume they check them out.

I started building up a relationship with local area homeschoolers back in 2018–2019. Throughout the fall of 2019 and early 2020, I was planning a Homeschool Information Night in which 10 to 12 local area homeschool co-ops and other resources (i.e., a representative from Elgin Community College) had a mini expo in the library's big meeting room.

Coronavirus hit and ruined all our plans, but, when August 2020 rolled around and the concept of school was very strange, I contacted all those people again to see if they could do a webinar the following week. Having those existing connections was essential to throwing together a webinar with just days of notice. The live webinar was kind of successful, but the views of the recording on YouTube were very successful.

I am a part of the School District 300 Discussion group on BFB (I am not a parent, just in the group for professional reasons) and noticed it was heavy on parents posting about pulling their kids from school. The McHenry County Homeschool Happenings BFB group was adding hundreds of new parents each week, and they were all posting about knowing nothing about homeschooling or being intimidated, looking for COVID-19 homeschool parent advice. There seemed to be a community need for something, anything on this topic.

Scholastic Teachables also offered me a deal I couldn't refuse in July, and our patrons have been using it consistently. August 2020 was particularly high in use for that.

Holly Eberle, MLIS
Youth Technology Librarian
Algonquin Area Public Library District

Association for Library Services to Children (ALSC)

ALSC, a division of ALA, "believes that all children, no matter their circumstances or attributes, need and deserve the very best opportunities, and envisions a future where public libraries are recognized as vital to all children and communities that support them."[1] This support is regardless of parental choice, school choice, and home life. *All* youth deserve to have opportunities presented to them and advocated for by the public library. The core competencies set forth by ALSC are all relevant to the at-home learner population. The ALSC competencies expound upon the role of a children's librarian in the community and professionally.[2]

The ALSC Core Competencies include:

- commitment to client group reference and user services
- programming skills; knowledge
- curation, and management of materials
- outreach and advocacy
- administrative and management skills
- professionalism and professional development

Young Adult Library Services Association (YALSA)

YALSA, a division of ALA, has a vision that all teens from a variety of backgrounds, including, but not limited to ability, class, gender identity, sexual orientation, race, religion, and power-differentiated groups, will have access to quality library programs and services—no matter where they occur—that are tailored to the community and that create new opportunities for all teens to promote personal growth, academic success, and career development, while linking teens and staff to resources, connected learning opportunities, coaching, and mentoring.[3]

YALSA recently revised the Teen Services Competencies for Library Staff:

- Teen Growth and Development: Knows the typical benchmarks for growth and development and uses this knowledge to plan, provide, and evaluate library resources, programs, and services that meet the multiple needs of teens.
- Interactions with Teens: Recognizes the importance of relationships and communication in the development and implementation of quality teen library services and implements techniques and strategies to

support teens individually and in group experiences to develop self-concept, identity, coping mechanisms, and positive interactions with peers and adults.
- Learning Environments (formal and informal): Cultivates high-quality, developmentally appropriate, flexible learning environments that support teens individually and in group experiences as they engage in formal and informal learning activities.
- Learning Experiences (formal and informal): Works with teens, volunteers, community partners, and others to plan, implement, and evaluate high-quality, developmentally appropriate formal and informal learning activities that support teens' personal and academic interests.
- Youth Engagement and Leadership: Responds to all teens' interests and needs and acts in partnership with teens to create and implement teen activities and to foster teen leadership.
- Community and Family Engagement: Builds respectful, reciprocal relationships with community organizations and families to promote optimal development for teens and to enhance the quality of library services.
- Cultural Competency and Responsiveness: Actively promotes respect for cultural diversity and creates an inclusive, welcoming, and respectful library atmosphere that embraces diversity.
- Equity of Access: Ensures access to a wide variety of library resources, services, and activities for and with all teens, especially those facing challenges to access.
- Outcomes and Assessment: Focuses on the impact of library programs for and with teens and uses data to inform service development, implementation, and continuous improvement.
- Continuous Learning: Acts ethically, is committed to continuous learning, and advocates for best library practices and policies for teen services.[4]

Textbox 5.1
Extending Teacher Cards to Homeschool Families
Librarian Cathy Bakken from Spokane Public Library in Spokane, Washington, says, "We've served homeschoolers with events since 2017. We created a homeschool card without fees or fines in 2018, though by 2020, we had no fines for anyone. We have done monthly events at three of our branches, took a break for COVID-19, and started up with Zoom events in October 2020."

Homeschool SERVICES

The Mount Prospect Public Library welcomes homeschooling families in the community and supports you through services, materials, and programs. The Parent/Teacher Collection in Youth Services has more than 2,000 titles. This collection contains many resources specifically chosen to help parents, caregivers, teachers, and librarians plan curricula and programming for students and families. We also have an extensive list of online web resources to support your homeschool needs.

Getting Books from the Library

The Mount Prospect Public Library offers Book Bag checkouts for homeschool families. Materials are checked out on your library card. Depending on the opening phase of the library, homeschool families can either pick up items via Parking Lot Pickup if the building is closed or in person at the library.

Book Bag Service

- Loan period is three weeks. Renewals may be possible by notifying the library in advance of the due date. Items that have holds cannot be renewed.
- Book bags contain approximately 15-25 items. Some topics may be limited to 5-10 books when in high demand.
- Homeschoolers are limited to one Book Bag at a time.
- To submit book bag requests: bookbag@mppl.org or 847-590-3320.
- Please allow 72-hours notice for all book bag requests.

Virtual Storytime Visits

Virtual storytimes for homeschool families are available September through May using Zoom. With a two-week notice, we are happy to tailor a storytime around your curriculum needs. To schedule, please contact Amy Slagter: 847-253-5675 or aslagter@mppl.org.

NEW Online Resources!
- *PebbleGo* by Capstone
- *Bookflix* from Scholastic
- *E-books* from RBdigital
- *StoryCove Folk and Fairytales*

Go to bit.ly/MPPLekids

Tutor.com® is an online program that connects students in kindergarten through high school with expert tutors in math, science, social studies, and English. For online homework and study assistance, students can access a tutor with their MPPL card between the hours of 2-9 p.m. daily at mppl.org/tutor. Up to five free sessions per card per week are offered in English and Spanish.

Special Collections

STEAM Kits

Supplement your science curriculum with fun and educational kits. STEAM kits contain a manipulative and a correlating book. Examples of kits include:

- Binoculars
- Insects—Four different insect specimens
- Weight & Volume—Use balance buckets to test, measure, and compare objects
- Reptangles—Assemble your own geometric masterpiece
- Building with Keva Planks
- Tracing—Write, trace, or draw your favorite designs then press a button and do it again with a Boogie Board Play n'Trace
- Drums
- Tangrams
- Bird Sounds

Science-to-Go Kits

Add some excitement to your lesson with kits that may include information, lesson suggestions, and equipment to perform activities. Search our catalog for list and availability at mppl.org and type in "science to go kits."

Tech Time Totes

These kits were created to provide quality tips and materials for children and adults to use together. Doing so will help children develop a healthy relationship with technology. Tech Time Totes can be checked out for three weeks; holds and renewals are allowed. These kit themes are available:

- Animals
- Colors
- Leaping Into Reading
- Letters
- Numbers
- On the Move
- Shapes
- Silly Stories
- Transportation

For more great information, check out
mppl.org/homeschool

 Mount Prospect Public Library
explore the opportunities

10 South Emerson Street • Mount Prospect, IL 60056
847-253-5675 • www.mppl.org

Figure 5.1. Mount Prospect Public Library Homeschooling Brochure. Mount Prospect Public Library.

The homeschool programs can be offered during the school day. We must meet our patrons where they are with what we have. If that means offering an educational program twice—once during a school day and once after a traditional school day—do it. Do it if the library has the staffing, resources, and stamina to do so. There is a growing trend of librarians and libraries offering teacher privileges to home educators. Usually, this is extended checkout periods, no fines, and services designed for the at-home learner.

The Mount Prospect Public Library (MPPL) near Chicago, in Mount Prospect, Illinois, has extended book bag services, story times, and virtual visits to homeschooling groups and additional educational offerings. The MPPL has a parent–teacher collection with over 2,000 items that can be tied to a curriculum. They offer book bag services, with a custom-created item selection of 15–25 items that can be requested three days before pick up.

Program planning librarians might find this teacher–librarian collaboration form helpful when planning and connecting with teachers and homeschool teachers. Back when I was teaching it was recommended to use a tangible form to document and track the teacher and librarian's collaboration. The following form I developed when I was an elementary district librarian. I used it when working with teachers and then submitted it with my lesson plans. I also gave a copy to the teacher. While it may seem old-fashioned in 2021, the form can be a shared living document for both the librarian and teacher. It streamlined communication in a busy school environment when conversations from the lunchroom might get lost. Feel free to adjust the form for and to your community!

Sidebar 5.2   Let's Collaborate!
Teacher and Librarian Needs Assessment

- What are you working on this week?
- What are you working on next week?
- Do you have a new unit coming up and would like help?
- Do you have a unit/lesson that involves research?
- Do you need help integrating technology?
- I want help, but I am not sure with what yet.
- Would you like books pulled on a topic? If yes, what topic?
- Would you like a pathfinder of websites? If yes, what topic?

Teacher/Librarian Collaboration Form

Date: Librarian: Teacher: Grade: Topic:	Topic expansion: The Librarian will: The Teacher will:
Pre-Search *Choose a topic for research *Create a keyword list *Establish a focus *Read for a focus/exploratory *Identify a problem *Brainstorm	
Research *Ask further questions *Explore information *Gather information *Read for information *Take notes	
Organize and Analyze *Locate sources (library/databases/websites) *Read for analysis *Compare/Contrast *Analyze information *Organize information	
Create, Expand, Present or Post *Write/Record *Product creation *Submit/Post/Present/Share *Revise/Edit	
Reflect and Evaluate *Evaluate sources/websites *Critique work *Reflect on project/process	
Cite *Citing Source *Create a works-cited Bibliography	
Book Talk	

*Pull books per assignment *Book Talk on selected items

Please select: __Pre-Search __Research __Organize & Analyze __Create/Expand/Present/Post __Reflect & Evaluate __Cite __Book Talk

Standard:

Purpose:

Objectives:

Activity:

Assessment:

End Product:	Resources:	Equipment:	Scheduling:

Librarian Reflection and Follow up:

Figure 5.2. Teacher Library Collaborations Form Christina Giovannelli-Caputo developed to use in a school library system. Christina Giovannelli-Caputo.

Rethinking the Library's Role in the Community

Robert Greenleaf coined the term "servant leadership," which first made its official debut in 1970 in the essay "The Servant as Leader." The notion is that to lead you must serve first. Perhaps that same is true for librarianship. "The servant-leader is the servant first. . . . It begins with the natural feeling that one wants to serve, to serve first," wrote Robert K. Greenleaf.

To lead the way, librarians must serve. As librarians, we often talk about serving our populations; naturally, we are servant-leaders not in the sense that another human being owns us but in the sense that we serve the community for the greater good. Greenleaf's website, accessed in 2021, states that

"A servant-leader focuses primarily on the growth and well-being of people and the communities to which they belong. While traditional leadership generally involves the accumulation and exercise of power by one at the 'top of the pyramid,' servant leadership is different. The servant-leader shares power, puts the needs of others first, and helps people develop and perform as highly as possible."[5] Greenleaf declared in his second essay, "The Institution as Servant," that an organization can instill servant leadership as well. He had great faith, according to his website, that organizational servant leadership could change the world.

It is 2021, and the mindset is in dire need to change from library worker to public worker. You might be wondering what the difference is. Librarians serve the community. Librarians are community helpers who are attendants to the public. Librarians are not only serving the brick-and-mortar walls of the library. Servant leadership is an interesting concept when applied to librarianship. As librarians, we serve the community—I am a youth services librarian. Youth *services*. Service. Serve. Servant. Maybe we need to rethink library services and library positions. Are we library servants (workers) or public servants (workers), and what is the difference?

Public servants focus on the communities' needs and community members' needs:

- Listening to the community
- Outreach within community
- Identifying issues and aligning the library resources to address community needs
- Building relationships with community partners to empower community

Library servants focus on the library building and the "stuff" in the facility:

- Telling the community how great we are
- Promoting the books and materials we selected
- Hosting programs featuring our items

It sounds like libraries and librarians are public servants that serve the community faithfully. At-home learners are heavy library users that often go unserved, without services specifically presented and provided for them.

The Library Can Fit the Homeschoolers' Needs

Education has been highly visible throughout the COVID-19 pandemic. Pandemic schooling is a "new normal," where more and more families are deciding to educate from home. Remote learning as a learning methodology does not have much leeway or ability to differentiate instruction. While remote or eLearning may be working for some families, for many of them, it is not. Home education is a long-forgotten option for schooling. Libraries have also been thrust into the spotlight during this educational crisis since libraries and education go hand in hand.

Recently, my family of six met two other homeschooling families, consequently not at a homeschooling co-op. Both families live near us in large suburbs of Chicago in what are "good" school districts. A year ago, this may not have been the case. Pandemic (home) schooling is undoubtedly on the rise. In 2019, estimations were holding firm, with 3.5 percent of all school-aged youth being homeschool. Now, I predict that, in districts where remote learning is solely taking place, 20 percent of all school-aged youth are home educated, an estimation based on my opinions through my associations and research. Dr. Brian Ray recently updated his research from January 2021: "There were an estimated 4.5 to 5.0 million homeschool students in grades K–12 in the United States during March of 2021 (roughly 8 percent to 9 percent of school-age children). There were about 2.5 million homeschool students in spring 2019 (or 3 percent to 4 percent of school-age children). The homeschool population had been growing at an estimated 2 percent to 8 percent per annum over the past several years, but it grew drastically from 2019–2020 to 2020–2021."[6]

It is imperative to create partnerships and develop relationships with the homeschool groups local to your library. There is a tremendous uptick in DIY schooling; libraries have the tools to support education. The question is, while there are homeschool groups in the area of your library serves, they may not want the help of the library—but more likely than not, they will welcome the resources and support. Building relationships is a lot like dating, two people getting to know each other, each seeing if the connection is right for them. The same goes for community engagement; the library needs to go to the community. We need to meet the community where they are—outside of the walls of the library. You see, the library can provide the most innovative and wonderful services; however, if the library does not have ties and partnerships with the community, the attempts are futile. Hence, when building a homeschool program, it is important to meet the homeschool community. Please get to know them, find out what the information needs

74 ∼ Chapter Five

are, and cater to them. A simple online search will yield local homeschool groups. Social media also is an effective way to meet groups—Facebook, Instagram, MeetUp, and so on. Send a message and ask to go to the group. Offer to do story time and bring crafts. It does not have to be a huge, fancy

Ages 7-12

TAKE AND MAKE: Homeschool: Keith Haring Action Figures Art Project

Explore colorful action figures inspired by pop artist Keith Haring and discover ways to create your unique masterpiece that will POP!

Find the video at: ppld.librarymarket.com/homeschool-keith-haring-action-figures

Supplies Included: Action figure template, guided drawing sheet, colored cardstock (half sheets), white drawing paper, bubble wrap, packing peanuts

From Home: Markers (colors and a black permanent), tempera or acrylic paints (optional), pencil, scissors, glue

Drawing the Figures (Two Different Ways)

1. Cut out your templates and use them to trace the figures onto colored cardstock. Cut out your colored cardstock figures. These are the figures you'll use in your project.

2. Or ... use the guided drawing sheet to draw your own figures on the colored cardstock and cut them out. You can also draw from observation (looking at the figures) and your imagination!

*You might want to start with pencil, but be sure to go over your outlines using a black marker that makes a bold line. Cut near the outside edge of the black line.

Create the Background (Three Ideas)

The white drawing sheet is the background paper. You can use markers or paints to create the background.

1. Draw a line across the paper, starting about a hand's width from the bottom. Make it bold using a black marker. This is the foreground. You can use markers or paint to fill in the foreground and background (above the line) using two contrasting colors. You could also add a simple design in the foreground, like Keith Haring ... black dash marks or a black line doodle design.

2. Or ... using a craft paint (tempera or acrylic), paint the sheet of bubble wrap. A primary color makes this Pop Art POP! Carefully lay the blank white sheet of drawing paper on top of the bubble wrap and gently "massage." Be careful not to let the paper slide around. Carefully lift the paper off the bubble wrap and set aside to dry.

3. Or ... try making a black line "doodle" design that covers the solid white paper, another Keith Haring favorite.

program offering, though it can be if you want. The group's parents and moderators may tell you what they are studying, which is helpful when planning a program.

Composing Your Masterpiece (Two Ideas)

When the background is ready, place your action figures on the paper, arranging them the way you want to glue them down. **If you drew in a foreground line, try making part of each figure touch inside the foreground.** That will make them look like the FOCUS of your project. Leave them in place and glue down one at a time, using one of the following ideas.

1. If you want the figures to really POP, glue a packing peanut to the back of each figure, then glue the packing peanut to the background. This gives your piece dimension.
2. Or … just glue the figures directly to the background!

*Your figures can be placed anywhere on your paper. They can tell a story or just show lots of action. This works well if you made a background using bubble wrap or doodles!

Making Them ACTION FIGURES:

Now that everything is in place, you can add the **MARKS THAT SET THE FIGURES IN MOTION**! See the samples below to get some ideas for placing your marks, using a black marker.

SOME SAMPLES TO INSPIRE YOU!

Check out other projects at: ppld.org/kids/create/whats-new

Figure 5.3. Pikes Peak Public Library District Homeschool Take and Make Flyer. Pikes Peak Public Library District.

Pikes Peak Public Library District (PPLD) from Colorado Springs, Colorado, has a two-room homeschool hub that houses educational materials, curricula, and a plethora of resources. PPLD has a large widely vast and varying homeschool programming offering, including a homeschool art show, homeschool cooking classes, science classes, STEM activities, a science fair, take and makes, and so on. The Madison Public Library from Madison, Wisconsin, offers teacher cards where DIY home educators can attain a teacher card to check out items that are intended for classroom use. These items can be checked out for six weeks and renewed up to five times with no overdue fines! The public library has tools and resources to support the AEMs that are in the community.

Cynthia Jennings a library director from Old Town Public Library, in Old Town, Maine, supports the library and homeschoolers. Jennings, a former homeschooling parent and a founding member of HOOT (Homeschoolers of Old Town), in 2007 wrote, "Homeschoolers and Public Libraries: A Synergistic Relationship." In the article Jennings wrote, "As a former home educator, I am certain it would have been impossible to educate my children without the wealth of resources available at our public library. As a public library director, I believe the energy and vibrant curiosity that home-educated children have, and the commitment and support their parents contribute, make libraries a better place for all."[7]

Notes

1. Created by the ALSC Education Committee, 1989; revised by the ALSC Education Committee, 1999, 2009, 2015, and 2020; and approved by the 2020 ALSC Board of Directors.

2. American Library Association, "Competencies for Librarians Serving Children in Libraries," November 30, 1999, accessed March 12, 2021, http://www.ala.org/alsc/edcareeers/alsccorecomps.

3. American Library Association, "Mission, Vision & Impact Statements," http://www.ala.org/yalsa/aboutyalsa/mission%26vision/yalsamission.

4. American Library Association, "Teen Services Competencies for Library Staff," March 1, 2010, accessed March 12, 2021, http://www.ala.org/yalsa/guidelines/yacompetencies.

5. Robert K. Greenleaf Center for Servant Leadership, https://www.greenleaf.org/.

6. B. Ray, "Homeschooling: The Research," https://www.nheri.org/research-facts-on-homeschooling/.

7. Cynthia Jennings, "Homeschoolers and Public Libraries: A Synergistic Relationship," *Maine Policy Review* 22, no. 1 (2013): 92–93, https://digitalcommons.library.umaine.edu/mpr/vol22/iss1/22.

CHAPTER SIX

Homeschool Programs and Outreach

Public libraries and library staff are an important part of an at-home learner's education. The public library can provide home-educated youth with an array of diverse learning materials, specialized programming, and focused subject experts. The library also houses study rooms, circulating technology and STEM items, craft supplies, and so much more.

There is a need for the local library to create strong partnerships with the homeschooling community. There are homeschooling families in all the communities that our libraries serve. Previous chapters have touched upon alternative educational methods (AEMs), which looked at the different philosophies and definitions of homeschooling. Essentially, teaching and learning are happening outside of traditional classroom walls, and often teaching is done in the home by the primary caregiver. This book is being written during COVID-19; the recommended practices in making connections and providing at-home learners services may change or be altered to fit the needs. Creating strong partnerships between the schooling community and the library will benefit the community by extending resources. Outreach and community engagement to the homeschooled audience and outreach and engagement within the library walls are essential to building the at-home learner collaboration.

In a 1998 article in the *Journal of Youth Services in Libraries*, Jane Kleist-Tesch states, "Homeschoolers rely heavily on public libraries to provide them with the tools they need. Such resources include, but are not limited to, information on homeschooling, resources for creating and carrying out curriculum, and legal materials. They also need services such as tours and story programs."[1]

Years ago, when I was building the homeschool and library partnership, I learned of a homeschool group that met at a park walking distance to the library where I served. I saw an opportunity to expand outreach efforts and gage interest in a collaborative relationship. So, I showed up- my kids in tow, completely unconventional.

I would bring my business cards, random leftover crafts, an assortment of advanced reader copies (ARCs), library swag, etc. The families were able to engage with me informally, and I met them where they were in the community. I would segue into what the library and subject experts could do for them. Some of the testimonials in this book are from relationships that I fostered personally. I urge you to think outside of the box.

Historically, public libraries are extensions of education, and librarians have always been innovative collaborators. Public libraries must make meaningful connections with homeschool youth and families. The following are steps I created to build an at-home learner community relationship through servant leadership at the library.

1. Identifying homeschool groups and organizations local to the library is the first step to providing effective homeschool services and programs. Engage in conversations with known at-home learners in the community, and if the library is unaware of who the homeschoolers are, pay attention while on the service desk. Homeschoolers and at-home learners will visit the library during a traditional school day; invite them to share experiences, join an advisory group, give your contact information, offer fun programming, and begin to foster a relationship. A simple online search for local homeschool groups might yield successful results. Email, call, stop by the groups (when safe again), and introduce yourself.
2. The second step is to learn about homeschooling in the community that the library serves. It is essential to learn about the community and its needs. One way to identify their needs is to organize a Homeschool Advisory Team where parents and youth can advise the library of their needs and identify ways to serve them. A needs assessment is another way to learn about this population's desires; an online survey tool like Survey Monkey, Google Survey, or a paper survey can do this. A needs assessment will help guide librarians in what the essentials are, along with intentional programming. It is essential to meet the homeschoolers in their environment.

3. Embed your library within the local homeschool community. Listen, Engage, Repeat. These opportunities will bring library resources to a group that is historically heavy library users but have different informational needs of a traditionally educated adolescent. Only after the partnerships are formed between the local organizations and the library can they begin working together to offer the best services to fit the group's homeschooling needs.
4. Once groups and organizations are identified, contact them, and inquire if they are interested in having a representative from the library attend as a guest presenter virtually or in person (when safe). Perhaps the library point person can attend a homeschool co-op once a month, September through May, or an optimum timetable for both parties. After the schedules between the co-ops and library are established, the guest staff member might bring materials to the groups, talk about programs at the library, book talk, share new items, bring STEM activities, or present a story time.

Makerspaces and Library of Things (LOT)

The communities at home learners will treasure homeschool workshops in the makerspace and extended checkouts with Library of Things (LOT). The past decade has been full of progress for public libraries, with the advent of makerspaces that extend services into the community. At the core of the makerspace ethos is the idea of engaging the community. Makerspace services can span all ages, socioeconomic classes, education, and experience levels to provide a shared learning space. The trend of makerspaces and digital creation labs in libraries indicates the evolving library space, focused on experience, creation, and learning.[2] The birth of makerspaces and infusion of local partnerships provide communities with innovative experiences.

Libraries are transformative and essential for all types of learners. Makerspaces typically have expensive equipment that might be beyond the reach of a homeschool family to own. Homeschoolers will happily utilize the 3D printers, woodcutter, sewing machine, industrial kitchen, and more. Extending the training and programming of the makerspace materials to schooling institutions will foster community education! LOT and homeschoolers go hand in hand. While makerspaces host the equipment, the LOT circulates the equipment.

Textbox 6.1
"STEAM materials can be particularly cost-prohibitive for families, so some libraries purchase these items to be circulated. The Matteson Area Public Library has Dash Robot, 3D pens, Cubelets, Snap Circuits, and microscopes. STEAM kits are a way that libraries can create learning experiences for their younger patrons. Skokie Public Library has STEAM kits on such subjects as robotics, music, measurement, fossils, coding, and more, with accompanying short YouTube videos that provide an overview of the kits. Circulation of these items varies depending on the library, with some allowing them to be borrowed by those with reciprocal access and others only allowing cardholders to use the materials." —Jennifer Robertson, Carbondale Public Library[3]

There are a handful of studies and surveys regarding making connections with homeschoolers by the public library. In 1991, Robin Schwartz posed an exploratory research survey for the home-educating community about their students' use of public library resources.[4] The survey was distributed to over 2,000 Ohio families in the homeschool community. The results still hold true in 2021. "There are several services homeschoolers would like public libraries to offer: (1) to receive the same treatment as public school teachers, with the right to check out larger numbers of materials for longer periods of time; (2) to provide more religious (Christian) materials; (3) to provide additional information and books about homeschooling; (4) to give more assistance in book selection and library orientation; (5) to foster positive relationships between library staff and homeschoolers; (6) to supply more computer equipment and software, and instruction in their use."[5]

It is recommended to survey the learning community. The homeschooling audience has expanded to include at-home learners and COVID-19 homeschoolers. The learning environment and AEMs are fluid, constantly changing with the need of the times. The survey will drive community and learning engagement specific to your library. Upon fostering and building relationships, administer the survey to all learning institutions and environments in the community. Once that has been established, the library can evaluate the survey results and program from there. Each library's community will have unique schooling and learning needs. This is the reason surveying and community engagement are necessary to effectively serve. There is no one size fits all approach to education, and there is no one size fits all approach for surveys or programming. What do at-home learners and homeschoolers want from the library?

- To be close
- Circulating items
- Library and literacy skills
- Online databases
- Space and support
- Educational programs

Sidebar 6.1
"I remember the libraries from my childhood very fondly. My mom would take my brothers and me every week, and sometimes we would make several trips in that time. I loved the library and utilized it in many ways. I was an avid reader, so often I would read after I finished my schooling for the day. Because we visited so often, the library ended up being an instrumental part of not only my academic life but my personal and social well-being as well.

First, the library was able to supplement my homeschooling simply because I digested so many books. I would come home with novels, which helped with my own writing abilities and vocabulary. I wouldn't have had access to all those books and information without the public library. The library also often offered programs that encouraged us to read, with rewards to encourage reading. In this sense, the library allowed me to have fun life experiences like going to Six Flags Great America or the Raging Waves Water Park, experiences that I would probably not have had access to otherwise. The library also usually offers discounts on museums, aquariums, zoos, and other fun and educational places with a high price tag. For those reasons, I think the library was very helpful to my education and personal well-being." —Madison, a homeschooled youth from Chicago on the library

---

Programs for At-Home Learners

Local and national public libraries recognize the growing population of homeschooling families within their communities and extend school service amenities to them. As librarians who often work in a customer-facing role and a service desk, we are aware of creating positive customer experiences. It is important to provide inviting library spaces and foster welcoming encounters for our patrons. All reference questions matter and are important. All schooling diversity questions are important and should be met with the same enthusiasm and personalization that we as public service desk staff typically employ to a reference interview. The service desk serves as a conversation starting point, as it is a natural way to meet at-home learners and homeschooled youth; pay attention when the youth are in the library. Families that home educate and youth who school at home often talk among each other, and positive encounters at the library will be shared within the homeschool circle.

The library employs innovative subject experts. One such expert, Kary Henry, the school outreach coordinator from Deerfield Public Library in Deerfield, Illinois, presents an incredible array of homeschool library programs. She is a well-known blogger for the American Library Association's Association for Library Service to Children blog. Henry offers programming biweekly for the homeschooling families: Homeschool Hangout, Homeschool Book Club, and Homeschool @ the Library. One of the programs is for youth 7 to 10 years old and another for youth 11 to 14.

Collaboration efforts should include fostering cross-departmental outreach and engagement to offer a broad range of programs and services. I call it "collective inner library partnerships" that support working together and reaching goals for the community's common good. It is a form of outreach and engagement within the library itself while thinking about the community's needs. Provide staff training, as staff in other departments may not be as fluent about at-home learners. Provide training opportunities for all departments to acquire knowledge about the learners in the community, live or recorded. Start with the legalities of education per the state level, distinguish the differences in schooling options, share the local homeschool groups, and lobby for how the library can serve the audience.

Homeschool Advisory Team

"Homeschool Advisory Team" (HAT) is enlisting the homeschooled parents in the area to give direct feedback on the type of homeschool programming the at-home learner community needs. It is important to listen to this audience, as their informational needs will differ from that of a traditional educated youth. Youth enrolled in brick-and-mortar schools may be receiving library informational curriculum via the school. At-home learners and homeschoolers, however, may not be. Be aware and mindful of the different informational needs when brainstorming and programming. Begin by starting HAT, marketing it in the newsletters, website, and social media. Ask for the parents to advise, and they will. These parents are invested in

Homeschool Programs and Outreach

their youths' education; they will join forces with the library to expand literacies.

You must come to these meetings prepared. It is entirely acceptable to want to have an open plan, but have an agenda for these meetings. Offer the meetings during a variety of times, at night, weekends, and even during the weekday. Make the connection. Likely, the library will have a teen advisory board (if your library does not, perhaps think of starting one), and offering a homeschool advisory group is a natural step. HAT can cater to the youth or the parents.

Homeschool Jam Session

I partnered with Bryan Bednarek, who at the time was the Digital Media Specialist at Arlington Heights Memorial Library (AHML) to offer "Homeschool Jam Session." AHML has an onsite recording studio and a digital media lab! Homeschool Jam Session was a spin-off of a previously established program, and we offered it during the school day for homeschool teens. The teens learned how to use the recording studio and wrote and recorded an original song in 90 minutes with vocals and instruments. It was incredible to work with a brilliant colleague at a different service point and learn about other departments while providing a needed program to homeschoolers.

Figure 6.1. Teens learn how to use studio equipment during the Homeschool Jam Session Program. Christina Giovannelli-Caputo.

Figure 6.2. Teens learn how to use studio equipment during Homeschool Jam Session Program. Christina Giovannelli-Caputo.

Lunch Bunch

Homeschool Lunch Bunch was created in direct response to a customer request. A few years ago, a patron requested on a homeschool survey that the library would offer a program with a public speaking aspect for homeschoolers. "Lunch Bunch Show-and-Tell" was the brainchild of that request. The premise of the program is that of a brown-bag lunch and show-and-tell. There is no cost to hosting this program other than staff time. There is no age limit; ours was open to all grades and levels. Lunch Bunch could easily be divided by age or grade. The program is held during lunchtime hours. The youth brought their lunch, ate together, and shared objects or talking points important to them, big or small, a basic show-and-tell.

Homeschool Hangout

"Homeschool Hangout" is a laid-back, easygoing program. It is scheduled once a month for two hours during the school day, September through May, from 1:00 p.m. to 3:00 p.m. It can easily be replicated at any library if there are programming space and workforce. I recommend offering this program

Figure 6.3. Homeschooled youth at Homeschool Hangout. Christina Giovannelli-Caputo.

specifically to the home educated. I often bring the STEM kits and STEM activities to the program. Homeschoolers may not have the expensive equipment that traditional schooled youth have experienced. Offer microscopes, robots, Dash and Dot, coding materials, Lego Robotics, board games, and other technology for hands-on contact. You can have a theme with planned activities or have leftover crafts with a relaxed vibe. Customize the program to suit your homeschool community. Our typical Homeschool Hangout program is for all school-aged youth, younger siblings, and parents.

Behind the Scenes Library Tour

Homeschooled youth may not have had traditional brick-and-mortar library experiences with information literacy lessons. To kick off summer reading, I invited additional youth services staff to share behind-the-scenes information with homeschoolers. We toured the facility and stopped to talk to staff at various service points. Youth services staff shared the summer reading promotional materials given to local schools. A special tour of the bookmobile was the highlight of this series of programming. Youth were given information about the bookmobile from the staff. The homeschoolers learned how the bookmobile provides services to the community.

Homeschool Movie

Another easy and inexpensive program to offer is "Homeschool Movie." The premise and inspiration are to show an educational movie during the school day. Disney's "Nature Bears" was shown in the story time room on the projector. The only cost to this program was my time, and I ordered a new DVD on Blu-ray. Before COVID-19, a homeschooled youth requested for the library to host a movie club. The theme for the program was to be the Lion King. Once it is safe, I hope we will watch the movie together and discuss it as a group. To show movies in a public library, the library must have a license to not violate copyright laws. See "The Umbrella License® for Public Libraries" at https://library.mplc.org/.

National School Choice Week

"National School Choice Week" (NSCW; https://schoolchoiceweek.com/) is usually the last week of January and presents meaningful programming opportunities. The library may allow for display cases to be used by schools to market and recruit. School choice is evolving and growing—more families now than ever are embracing AEMs. School choice was viewed as far left and far right in the recent past, and now schooling diversity has become mainstream. The library is a bipartisan institution that serves the whole schooling community. There are likely AEMs in your community that diversify the audience—not all youth are schooled in the public system.

Homeschool 101

"Homeschool 101" is a parent-focused program that can be hosted in a panel forum. I have offered this program during NSCW. Best practices include extending invitations to different homeschool organizations and groups local to the library to speak about their organizations to prospective families. Here is a description of Homeschool 101 that I offered: "Find out how to begin your homeschool journey, learn about Illinois state laws regarding homeschooling, and get connected with local homeschool groups and resources in the northwest Chicago suburbs. There will also be a Q&A time at the end of the meeting to go over any specific questions. For parents; families welcome." Homeschool 101 programming can be focused to share information for potential homeschooler and at-home learner families; it also can be used to educate the community on schooling diversity and foster understanding. Kathy Wentz, from Wentz Educational Services, can be hired to present this program at the library as well (https://kathywentz.blogspot.com/p/workshops.html).

Homeschool Parents Night Out/ At-Home Learners Parents Night In

Seeing a need in the community for an expansion of services, I enlisted Bill Pardue, a digital services librarian at Arlington Heights Memorial Library. Pardue and I presented a program called "Homeschool Parents Night Out" where we presented on the educational resources the library offered and had to circulate. Pardue, a vibrant speaker, focused on the database and online content, which was hosted through the AHML.info website, while I focused on programming for homeschoolers, STEM kits, and circulating materials. I often invited Pardue to the Homeschool Hangouts for informal reference assistance and caregiver support.

The at-home learning and homeschool community needs the sustenance of the library and librarians. Pardue and I collaborated cross-departmentally to present "At-Home Learner Parents' Night In" (video of program is linked in the endnotes[6]). This was formerly an in-person program, presented as "Homeschool Parents Night Out" in years past. We reformatted the presentation to be hosted on Zoom, while focusing on the various services and resources the library offers. School District 25 (video is linked in the endnotes[7]) supported and promoted the program by interviewing both librarians and sharing via social media. Also, while it is difficult to directly attribute database usage changes to specific programs, there were significant increases in usage of Tumble Book Library read-alongs and Miss Humblebee's Academy's lessons completed in September, both of which were featured in the presentation. The comprehensive milieu of the library's collection, subject experts and staff, educational programs, and innovative space has endless engagement possibilities.

School Information Fair

Typical NSCW programming would include the Homeschool 101 program, but we could not host this in person in 2021 due to COVID-19. As a result, I proposed a new concept—Virtual School Information Night. This program was inclusive of all local schools that would like to participate.

> **Sidebar 6.2**
> "In pre-COVID times, one of the most heavily attended events that the library where I serve hosts annually is the Preschool Information Night. Daycare and preschool representatives are provided with booth space in the library, and hundreds of attendees cycle through to talk about the many options for their children's education. When it became obvious that the Preschool Information Night could not happen the same way this year, Christina saw the opportunity to adapt and expand the program to be a virtual School Information Fair for all education, birth through 12th grade. She enlisted Laura Dakas, youth services specialist, who normally runs the Preschool Information Night, and me, the youth outreach librarian, for my connection to the K–12 schools. We partnered with 40 daycares, schools, and homeschool co-ops from the surrounding areas to provide valuable information to caregivers. Each organization provided a link displayed in two collections on the Youth Services Wakelet, one for daycares and preschools and one for K–12 education, with almost 500 combined views. I encouraged the educators to create Bitmoji Classrooms to incorporate multiple links and hosted two virtual workshops to teach them how. Once the resources were gathered, parents had a week to view the Wakelets before a live Zoom event. During the event, representatives from the organizations were given their own breakout rooms. The 70 participants had an opportunity to visit the breakout rooms to ask questions of the representatives."
> —Emily Koch, youth outreach librarian from Arlington Heights Memorial Library

While my colleagues and I missed being in person with our schools and families, the virtual format allowed us to reach far beyond the standard attendees. Parents from all over were able to attend from the comfort of their homes. I spoke with a father during the program who was in Washington on a business trip, and he was looking for private schools for his children. If this had been an in-person program, he would have had to miss it due to travel. Hosting a Virtual School Information Fair is a beneficial program during and after COVID-19.

Homeschool Information at the Library

Have a section on the library's website explicitly devoted to at-home learners. Define what at-home learners and homeschoolers are and how the library can serve them. Link the webpage to various groups local to the

Figure 6.4. Johnsburg Public Library Homeschool Resource Center. Christina Giovannelli-Caputo.

Figure 6.5. Johnsburg Public Library Homeschool Resource Center. Christina Giovannelli-Caputo.

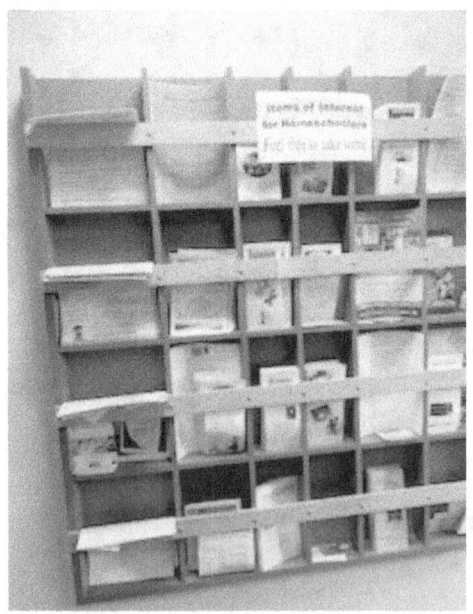

Figure 6.6. Johnsburg Public Library Homeschool Resource Center. Christina Giovannelli-Caputo.

library. If possible, include contact information to a staff person. A best practice is to have this same information available at the service desks for in-person customers.

The most famous and largest homeschool resource center in Illinois, and perhaps the US, is at Johnsburg Public Library. The library is home to the Homeschool Resources Center (HRC; https://www.johnsburglibrary.org/content/homeschool-resource-center). Kathy Wentz, a homeschooling parent, advocate, and library volunteer, applied for and received a $55,000 grant in 2001. Funding for this grant was provided by the Illinois State Library, a division of the Office of Secretary of State, using federal Library Services and Technology Act (LSTA) monies.[8] LSTA grants are to engage Illinois residents and communities through library technology, programs, and services to promote lifelong learning and services to persons having difficulty using libraries.[9] Wentz has 2,000 items in the HRC, a 12-foot by 12-foot room, and many programs and resources available year-round. At the HRC, there is an entire wall dedicated to homeschooling information. If you are local to the Midwest or have an HRC near you, take a staff field trip. This is how I met Kathy Wentz; I took a preplanned day trip to Johnsburg's HRC and asked to meet with her and for a tour!

Grayslake Public Library (https://www.grayslake.info/) in Grayslake, Illinois, offers specifically targeted homeschool programs. Colleen Ryan, the youth outreach assistant librarian and Grayslake resident home education specialist, supports the local community's home education audience. Grayslake Public Library holds a National Geographic Bee, which is usually very popular with homeschoolers. More information on the GeoBee can be found at https://www.nationalgeographic.org/education/student-experiences/geobee/. Ryan said, "Having spent 20 years homeschooling my own four kids, I already understood how homeschoolers think. And since homeschoolers tend to utilize the library and library services pretty often, I had an idea how to help meet their needs."

Grayslake Homeschooling Programs include the following:

- Offer monthly (September–May) support group meetings for the parents. There are many co-ops and enrichment programs for the students, but not much available for parents. Cover topics like curriculum, learning styles, how to school multiple ages, and how to tackle homeschool and housework, and more. I try to balance, so some topics pertain to home education while others are practical regarding daily life.
- Host the National Geographic Bee every December. They love it!

- Offer a low-key public speaking program where students can talk about whatever topic intrigues them for 10 minutes.
- Every August, host a program *about* homeschooling. What are your state's laws? How to discern your child's learning style, what a typical day schedule looks like, and more.
- Provide an online form that parents can complete when studying a particular topic. The parent submits the topic, grades of their children, and types of resources they are interested in, and then I gather the resources together for them. All they need to do is come pick them up. It is an excellent service that they enjoy.
- Provide a packet containing information regarding Illinois state law, pros and cons of registering, how to transfer students from a public school to a private home school, and a host of other documents as well as various books and resources the library has on homeschooling.

Public librarians and libraries have a long history of community and school engagement. Host training sessions for library staff and the public to learn more about homeschooled youth in the community. Establish a point librarian or staff member for outreach relationships with the homeschool population. Extend amenities and be comprehensive in providing services for all. Homeschool families and youth will ecstatically welcome services and programs developed specifically for their community.[10]

Notes

1. J. M. Kleist-Tesch, "Homeschoolers and the Public Library," *Journal of Youth Services in Libraries* 11, no. 3 (1998): 231–41, http://web.a.ebscohost.com.proxy.ulib.uits.iu.edu/ehost/detail/detail?vid=8&sid=b7ecfce6-3820-4c8f-9a9a-c63eea1dae90%40sessionmgr4006&hid=4206&bdata=JnNpdGU9ZWhvc3QtbGl2ZQ%3d%3d#AN=502794971&db=lls.

2. Kristin Fontichiaro, "Creation Culture and Makerspaces," in *Information Services Today*, ed. Sandra Hirsh (Lanham, MD: Rowman & Littlefield, 2015), 192–98.

3. J. Robertson, "Libraries to the Rescue: Providing Homeschooling Support during a Pandemic," December 2020, https://www.ila.org/publications/ila-reporter/article/142/libraries-to-the-rescue-providing-homeschooling-support-during-a-pandemic.

4. R. Schwartz, "Ohio Home-Schooled Children and Their Use of Public Library Resources," Unpublished Master's Thesis (Kent State University, Kent, OH, 1991).

5. Ibid.

6. "At-Home Learners Parents Night In," YouTube, https://www.youtube.com/watch?v=oohuMGXVYpI&t=2s.

7. District 25 Promotional Video for At-Home Learners Parents Night In, https://www.facebook.com/watch/?v=386144772377139-.

8. K. Wentz, "Homeschool Resource Center," https://www.johnsburglibrary.org/content/about-homeschool-resource-center-hrc.

9. "Library Services Technology Act," https://www.cyberdriveillinois.com/departments/library/grants/lsta.html.

10. Christina Caputo, "Hanging with My Homies," *Voice of Youth Advocates VOYA*, September 2018–November 2019.

CHAPTER SEVEN

Growing Diversity in Home Education

A diverse group of education reformers has shaped home education; John Holt from the far left, the Moores from the far right, and between them many more. In 2019, Aaron Hirsh conducted a research-based piece on the "The Changing Landscape of Homeschooling in the United States." Hirsh focused on the changing demographics in homeschooling.[1] The once prominent Anglo schooling method has proven to be transitioning to a diversified movement in socioeconomic and cultural diversity and methodologies. The National Center for Educational Statistics (NCES) National Household Education Parent and Family Involvement (PFI) Survey collected data from kindergarten through grade 12 students. The data presented 8 percent of the students were of Black descent and 26 percent were of Hispanic descent.

The data from the National Household Education Survey (2016) provides an insight into the equivalent grade levels of homeschool students. The largest portion, 31 percent, is high school age; 24 percent are the equivalent of grades 6–8; 23 percent are grades K–2, and 22 percent are grades 3–5. The statistics reveal that the largest portion of homeschoolers is high school aged.[2]

The homeschool population your library serves ranges from birth to adult, early childhood through the college level, and beyond. Online college and university programs are on the rise, according to NCES data. All students who were registered entirely online rose to 15.4 percent (previously 14.7 percent in 2016), or about one in six students. Doug Lederman's article from 2018, "Online Education Ascends," states that one-third of all college

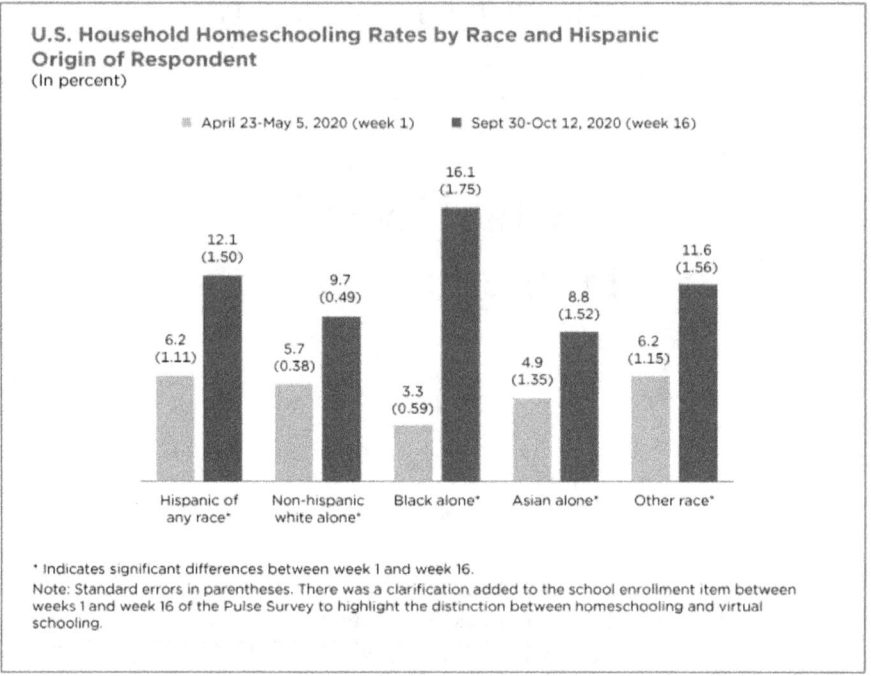

Figure 7.1. US Census Bureau Household Pulse Survey Weeks 1 and 16, Homeschooling Demographics during COVID-19. US Census Bureau.

students are taking at least one online course.[3] Online courses, virtual courses, and distance learning are all forms of home study.

A wide variety of families homeschool, including Muslims, Jews, Christians, Mormons, Atheists, conservatives, liberals, libertarians, military, families of all income levels, families of all ethnicities and color, and families of all education levels. Families of color are not alone in selecting alternative schooling and home education. While there are no hard and fast statistics (yet), initial studies show that LGBTQIA+ homeschool students are rising. Global Village School (https://www.globalvillageschool.org/lgbt.html) is one of many homeschooling organizations that support LGBTQIA+ students through alternative distance learning.

According to Movement Advancement Project (MAP), "Best estimates suggest that between 7–9 percent of youth identify as lesbian, gay, bisexual, transgender, or queer."[4] From these estimates, experts from the Williams Institute—a groundbreaking research institute on the LGBTQIA+ community and the law—predict that there are possibly 3.2 million LGBTQIA+ school-aged youths living in the US. The prediction from Williams Institute is that over 50 percent of those youth are people of color.⁵ While most LGBTQIA+ youths are traditionally schooled, there is an upswing in homeschooling numbers in this community. The unenrollment of an LGBTQIA+ student from a brick-and-mortar school might be for more varied and distinct reasons than was stated from the NCES PFI survey.

Idzie Desmarais is a well-known Canadian homeschool advocate in the LGBTQIA+ community and author of the 2008 book *I'm Unschooled. Yes, I Can Write*. She suggests the numbers of LGBTQIA+ youth might be higher than the Williams Institute estimation. "In my experience with the unschooling community specifically (not the broader homeschooling community), the percentage of children and teens identifying as LGBTQIA+ is . . . closer to 20 percent. I've speculated that one of the reasons for this is being part of a very accepting community, with parents working from a philosophy that's all about supporting the individual child for who they are, meaning that unschoolers are more likely to come out at a younger age. I'd also suspect that LGBTQIA+ children, being far more likely to feel ostracized and unwelcome in school . . . are more likely to be pulled out and unschooled/homeschooled than their straight/cisgender counterparts."⁶

In 2018, Gina Riley from Hunter College, located in New York City, New York, published the first of its kind study titled "A Qualitative Exploration of the Experiences of Individuals Who Have Identified as LGBTQIA+ and Who Have Homeschooled or Unschooled."⁷ The study focuses on 18 adults who identify as LGBTQIA+ and their homeschooling experiences for at least four years. The quote above from Desmarais is from Gina Riley's innovative study. There were four main beneficial commonalities that participants reported back on being homeschooled while identifying as LGBTQIA+ The benefits included more freedom and autonomy, breaking free from traditional (school) social norms, more time for education/exploration about sexuality and gender, and peer support from the LGBTQIA+ homeschooling community. The primary and sole challenge that they shared was a lack of available resources. While the internet has increased awareness and global social connections, community resources are always welcomed. Creating community resources, partnerships, and engagement are highly coveted from the library by at-home learners. There often are library districts, local library partners, and library systems creating local library-wide consortiums. Working together for the community, a local consortium, or a group for alternatively educated LGBTQIA+ might be beneficial and on the library's radar.

One of the survey questions Gina Riley asked the participants was, "What (if any) is your relationship between choosing to homeschool and being [LGBTQIA+]?"

Leaving school when I did (as well as the house I grew up in and the town I grew up in) hugely allowed me to come out to myself in the first place. I went to Not Back to School Camp and felt very supported in my questioning process through that community (both during the camp itself and maintaining those friendships/connections throughout the year), so I really doubt I would have come out to myself as a teen at all if I had stayed in public school. I think I would have stayed in denial as a coping mechanism, and I'm glad I didn't have to.

I felt I avoided a lot of social stigma and pressure (and bullying) by being homeschooled. I'm not sure if this has any effect on how comfortable I am with my queer identity now, but it's worth noting.[8]

Being responsive to the homeschooling community is imperative, says Amy Seto Forrester, a librarian from Colorado and former homeschooler and author of "Encouraging Educational Diversity Depictions of Homeschoolers in Middle-Grade Fiction." Forrester shares her experiences, "Just as librarians should seek to collect materials that reflect racial and cultural diversity, they should also seek to collect materials with educational diversity. Homeschooling culture is as richly diverse and vibrant as any other in the United States, and we should strive to reflect that in our collections."

A concept was born in the late 1980s by educator Emily Style. Style suggested that books provide windows into reality, not just imaginary worlds, and books that reflect a reader's own life are mirrors.[9] In 1990, educator Rudine Bishop added, books can be sliding glass doors, opening the door to experiences and allowing the reader to enter them. Bishop's writing, "Mirrors, Windows, and Sliding Glass Doors," explains that books are mirrors that reflect exposure to others so that reading becomes a means of self-confirmation or affirmation.[10] "Books are sometimes windows, offering views of worlds that may be real or imagined, familiar or strange. These windows are also sliding glass doors, and readers have only to walk through in imagination to become part of whatever world has been created or recreated by the author. When lighting conditions are just right, however, a window can also be a mirror," wrote Bishop.

It can be extremely powerful for all youth, especially marginalized youth, to see themselves and their experiences reflected positively in a book. A movement was born on Twitter, hashtag #Ownvoices, in 2015 by young adult author Corinne Duyvis. This movement has encouraged authors to share their own experiences through authentic stories.

Youth need diverse books. There is a need to have books that reflect similar experiences; it creates connections. Stories about cultures and races, sexual and gender identity, various family makeups, food insecurity and poverty, and even schooling diversity are essential. We Need Diverse Books (https://diversebooks.org/) is an organization with a mission to put books with diverse characters into the hands of youth. All youth should see themselves in a book. Home-educated youth need to see alternative education method protagonists in books they read. If homeschooled youth solely read books about traditionally educated students or distorted and negative homeschooled experiences, there is a good possibility they will begin to believe those views and become devalued.

The NCES reports the number of Hispanic homeschooled youth dramatically spiked from 2012 (265,000) to 2016 (444,000). This increase in homeschool numbers exceeds the enrollment development of Hispanic students in the public school sector. Surprisingly, there is little to no research on the Hispanic homeschoolers from scholars. It is staggering that over one-quarter of all US homeschoolers are Hispanic, so where is the research? The Florida Parent Educators Association noticed a rise in Hispanic families and an increase in homeschooling statewide.[11] A popular homeschool blogger, Monica Olivera, from Mommy Maestra (http://www.mommymaestra.com/), began her blog in 2010 to share homeschool content with other Latinx families. She shares on the blog a desire to instruct her children in a multilinguistic and bicultural method and a poor rating school system where her family lived as reasons for the jump to home education. The mission of Mommy Maestra is to help Hispanic families become involved in their child's education. Olivera has vocally paved the way for other Hispanic and Latinx families.

The 2003 study titled "Dismay and Disappointment: Parental Involvement of Latino Immigrant Parents" focuses on school-aged youths' parent involvement from a community that is 90 percent from Latin America.[12] The study addresses barriers to family engagement; communication was named as a dominant theme by many of the immigrant Latinx parents. A homeschool parent who wished to be left annoyomous shared why she was homeschooling her son: "Some of his teachers did not know the difference

Textbox 7.1
The Reyes family from Florida shares, "I only have 18 years to train them, and build good character, and build in forgiveness and kindness and service," Reyes said. "I understand the order of (traditional schooling), but it wasn't something for us. The things that were the most important to the school system weren't the most important things to me."

between Latinx cultures. Another teacher thought all the kids in his class came from Mexico. He needs to be taught his culture and the culture of his people by his people." Librarians and teachers need to recognize the ethnic variances within the Latinx population. Dr. Cheryl Fields-Smith, an expert in homeschooling in Black families, found there is no published research on homeschooling among Latinx and Spanish-speaking families.[13]

The National Black Home Educators (NBHE) organization was started in 2000 by Eric and Joyce Buges. The motto of NBHE is "Empowering Parents to Educate Children for Excellence," using free information and parental support. The NBHE hosts an annual national conference "that offers inspirational talks, practical how-to workshops, and useful resources for parents," says the website (https://www.nbhe.net/about-us/our-vision/). There is an annual fee of $75 per year per family as of 2020. The NBHE serves families across the US and globally.

Some families of color are hesitant to break free from the school system, due to the decades of fighting for desegregation and equal access. In "Morning by Morning: How We Home-Schooled Our African-American Sons to the Ivy League," Paula Penn-Nabrit recounts hostile feedback from relatives on why they chose to unenroll the boys from the traditional education model, especially since their uncle was instrumental in equal rights for Black students. James Nabrit alongside Thurgood Marshall, argued *Brown v. Board of Education* before the Supreme Court for equal educational opportunities. Penn-Nabrit's reasoning came down to school choice and doing what was best for her sons. She and her husband, both highly educated, schooled their songs from home in the subjects they felt comfortable teaching. They hired Black male tutors to teach the boys supplementally.

Studies indicate that Black families are a large growing homeschool group, citing reasons as low expectations for Black students and dissatisfaction with how their children—especially boys—are treated in schools. The National Black Home Educators (NBHE) organization was started in 2000 by Eric

---

Textbox 7.2

The legacy of the *Brown* decision is not only about access but is also about options. We African Americans owe it to our children to exercise all available opportunities to ensure their current and future success. We are not obligated to wait for schools to improve to better meet our needs; we are obligated to provide our children the best education available.
—Venus Taylor

and Joyce Buges. The motto of NBHE is "Empowering Parents to Educate Children for Excellence," using free information and parental support. The NBHE hosts an annual national conference "that offers inspirational talks, practical how-to workshops, and useful resources for parents," says the website (https://www.nbhe.net/about-us/our-vision/). There is an annual fee of $75 per year per family as of 2020. The NBHE serves families across the US and globally.

Black Family Homeschool Educators and Scholars (BFHES) was founded in 2020 by Black homeschool researchers Dr. Cheryl Fields-Smith and Dr. Khadijah Ali-Coleman. With the mission to engage the Black homeschooling community through, publications on scholarly research and community events for Black homeschoolers. BFHES has had two annual conferences, called Teach-Ins in 2020 and 2021. According to the website (http://blackfamilyhomeschool.org/about) BFHES is the first American based research and *education group* committed Black home education.

John Taylor Gatto, the author of *Dumbing Us Down* and other publications that were vocally against compulsory education, believed traditional education was and is systemically racist against youths of color. He believed in truth, justice, and freedom to learn, however, not in the compulsory fashion that is mainstream. Gatto challenged the status quo by deeming curriculum a form of brainwashing supremacy, forcing students to take on a subordinate social role. He claimed this especially resonated in Black communities as a form of modern slavery, the teacher the master and the student the slave. The teacher told the student what to read, how long to read it, what to learn, when to eat, when to run, and when to do everything for six hours a day. While Gatto, a critic of traditional education, was an advocate for youth autonomy of learning, he supported abolitionist educators who created alternative education methods (AEMs) to fit the need of the youth.

According to Gatto in *The Underground History of American Education*, "The backdrop of my teaching debut . . . was a predicament without any possible solution, a deadly brew compounded from twelve hundred black teenagers penned inside a gloomy brick pile for six hours a day, with a white guard staff misnamed 'faculty' manning the light towers and machine-gun posts. This faculty was charged with dribbling out something called 'curriculum' to inmates, a gruel so thin [that this school] might rather have been a home for the feeble-minded than a place of education."

Marva Collins, an American educator, created her teaching and schooling philosophy, which Gatto strongly supported. Collins, born in 1936, changed the face of education in urban Chicago. Growing up in the segregated South, she did not have access to a public library, and the schools had limited resources. Collins credits her father with her educational background; he supplemented her education at home with various readings and building her self-esteem. A formally schooled secretary during the 1950s, Collins found her way into the classroom in Chicago Public Schools (CPS). In CPS, she was hired to teach second grade. While she did not have a teaching certificate, she was hired due to a lack of applicants. With no formal training to teach, she trusted her instincts and disregarded the curriculum that focused on low-level readers and memorization drills in workbooks. Collins began to develop a method that worked with positive discipline (rather than punitive) and focused on phonics and teaching the students to think for themselves. After the 1968 riots in Chicago, the turnover rate for teachers and admin was high, and many fled to the Chicago suburbs. The incoming class of educators began teaching the standard educational curriculum, which Collins disregarded and rejected. Collins described the new teachers as "a different breed . . . who really didn't care or know what they were doing."[14] Collins's teaching philosophy was radically foreign to those that followed the standard and was objected to by the growing teachers' union. She resigned and began a new chapter in school choice and AEMs.

Collins independently taught a small group of youth for a year during the mid-1970s in Daniel Hale Williams University's basement while refining the method and honing her craft. She selected students labeled and forgotten by the system, teaching to their needs, and the youth bloomed in her love. Collins, confident in her teaching methods, withdrew over $5,000 from her teaching pension and turned the second floor of her home into a one-room schoolhouse. She was the first Black woman to start, own, and operate a private school independent from CPS. She supplied the school with desks and books bought as gently used and started the Westside Preparatory School (WPS). The WPS opened its doors in 1976 to 18 varying grade level students from low-income families who learned through phonics and the love of reading. She embodies a Socratic method—questioning and inspiring thought while respecting her students' uniqueness and intellectual freedom. Every day, Collins shared her love with the students, regardless if they disagreed with her. Collins helped them build their self-esteem, demonstrating they were worthy of love, creating a positive feedback loop, breaking the systemic educational scheme. She gained national acclaim through the mainstream media and a 1981 movie, *The Marva Collins Story*, and with the soaring achievement of high-risk youth, donations began to pour in. Collins eventually moved the schooling into a larger building that accommodated hundreds of youths. In 2008, she closed the doors to WPS; her legacy of teaching through love will live on forever.

Venus Taylor, author of "Behind the Trend: Increases in Homeschool among African American Families," is an unschooling mom of two and a Harvard graduate with a master's in education. She acknowledges the disparities in education by race and socioeconomic status. The exploratory US Census Bureau's Household Pulse Survey indicated that People of Color (POC) had the sharpest increase in homeschooling during COVID-19. POC are beginning to embrace their diverse schooling options and take control of their family's education. People have been conditioned to believe that public education is the sole opportunity, yet it is not. In the past, POC have been denied educational opportunities and access to quality schooling, while Brown was meant to change that, there are still significant achievement gaps between groups.[15] Indicating this drastic increase to home education is significant to society. People still want a choice and schooling is not a one size fits all. In 2008 and 2009, Cheryl Fields-Smith and Meca Williams innovatively studied Black homeschooling families' reasons, motivators, and beliefs for home education.

African American studies faculty member Marie-Josée Cérol—also known professionally as Ama Mazama at the Temple University in Philadelphia—began researching the growing trend of homeschooling in Black families. She began homeschooling her three children and found little to no information specific to Black families. Mazama conducted a report in 2012 in the *Journal of Black Studies*: "African American Homeschooling as Racial Protectionism."[16] The research and survey indicated that many families chose to "educate their children at home at least in part to avoid school-related racism." She also reports that American schools solely teach European and American history, with African history beginning during the Civil War. Along with the growing trend of Black families schooling at home, she teaches comprehensive African history, incorporating ancient African civilizations and in-depth about African people throughout history. Mazama believes this will grow a sense of self-esteem and racial pride in the African community.

In 2008 and 2009, Cheryl Fields-Smith and Meca Williams innovatively studied Black homeschooling families' reasons, motivators, and beliefs for home education. In the study called "Motivations, Sacrifices, and Challenges: Black Parents' Decisions to Home School," twenty-four Black homeschooling parents were engaged by surveys, interviews, and focus groups. Nineteen of the families deliberately infused and taught Afrocentric or Black American focused curricula.[17] Their report focused on two motivators for homeschooling. One was "the role of ethnicity"—"Black families perceived that institutional norms and structures within schools created destructive, rather than supportive, learning environments for children of African descent" (376). The other motivator was the "role of religion" (379). Many of the parents reported that religious beliefs influenced their decisions to homeschool. Some "directly shared a belief that God had actually led them to home schooling" while others "described home schooling as a complement and support to their religious beliefs" (379).[18]

There is a growing number of Muslim homeschoolers. Eaman Elhadri, the creator of "Muslim Homeschoolers Unite" at https://muslimhomeschoolersunite.com, is a teacher turned homeschooling mom. She shares on her website, "My education background has been beneficial in helping me create something I didn't have; something that we needed—the skill to integrate Islamic Studies into any secular subject and vice versa. . . . My passion is to equip Muslim families to homeschool in a way that is developmentally appropriate, spiritually nourishing, and based on proven methods of education." New Jersey has an active Muslim group called Muslim Homeschoolers at https://www.muslimhomeschoolers.org/. This group offers in-person groups often called in homeschooling jargon "co-ops." Muslim Homeschoolers website says, "Muslim Home Education has an unparalleled teaching method of Islamic principles and secular studies that prepares children for future success in this life and also the success in the afterlife." This group welcomes all and is inclusive while teaching Islamic principles.

There are homeschooling groups and families within all cultures, races, religions, and the community where your library serves. The diversity in schooling will be vast, and there is no one size fits all approach, as stated before. Make connections, learn about the local home education groups, and listen to what they need for developing services. Repeat those three steps to form a program within all marginalized communities.

The common denominator is that school choice, schooling diversity, and AEMs are welcomed in marginalized communities. Not all families learn the same way; not all families school, celebrate, or live the same way. We live in a beautifully diverse place that allows us the freedom to live and learn freely. The library can serve the vulnerable and home-educated marginalized learners. The diverse schooling community needs library subject experts and the library to offer services and space for groups to meet.

Notes

1. Aaron Hirst, "Changing Landscape of Education," https://www.crpe.org/sites/default/files/homeschooling_brief_final.pdf.

2. J. Redford, D. Battle, and S. Bielick, Homeschooling in the United States: 2012, NCES 2016-096REV (Washington, DC: National Center for Education Statistics, Institute of Education Sciences, US Department of Education, 2017).

3. D. Lederman, "Online Education Ascends," Inside Higher Ed, November 7, 2018, https://www.insidehighered.com/digital-learning/article/2018/11/07/new-data-online-enrollments-grow-and-share-overall-enrollment.

4. Movement Advancement Project, "Snapshot—LGBTQ by State," https://www.lgbtmap.org/LGBTQ-youth.

5. Williams Institute, https://www.law.ucla.edu/academics/centers/williams-institute.

6. G. Riley, "A Qualitative Exploration of the Experiences of Individuals Who Have Identified as LGBTQ and Who Have Homeschooled or Unschooled," Other Education, February 20, 2018, http://othereducation.org/index.php/OE/article/view/174.

7. Ibid.

8. Ibid.

9. E. Style, "Curriculum as Windows and Mirrors," The National SEED Project, accessed June 22, 2021, https://nationalseedproject.org/Key-SEED-Texts/curriculum-as-window-and-mirror.

10. R. S. Bishop, "Mirrors, Windows, and Sliding Glass Doors," *Perspectives: Choosing and Using Books for the Classroom* 6, no. 3 (1990).

11. Florida Parent Educators Association, https://fpea.com/.

12. A. F. Ramirez, "Dismay and Disappointment: Parental Involvement of Latino Immigrant Parents," *The Urban Review* 35, no. 2 (2003): 93–110.

13. C. Fields-Smith, "Homeschooling among Ethnic-Minority Populations," in *The Wiley Handbook of Home Education*, ed. Milton Gaither (Chichester, England: John Wiley and Sons, 2016), 207–21, https://doi.org/10.1002/9781118926895.ch9.

14. Marva Collins and Civia Tamarkin, *Marva Collins' Way*, fifth ed. (New York, NY: Penguin Putnam, 1990 [1982]), 32–38.

15. V. Taylor, "Behind the Trend: Increases in Homeschooling among African American Families," in *Home Schooling in Full View: A Reader*, ed. B. S. Coper (Greenwich, CT: Information Age Publishing, 2005), 121–33.

16. A. Mazama and G. Lundy, "African American Homeschooling as Racial Protectionism," *Journal of Black Studies* 43, no. 7 (2012): 723–48. https://doi.org/10.1177/0021934712457042.

17. C. Fields-Smith and M. R. Williams, "Sacrifices, Challenges and Empowerment: Black Parents' Decisions to Home School," *Urban Review* 41 (2009): 369–89.

18. Ibid.

CHAPTER EIGHT

The Future

The global spread of a virus became a pandemic in March 2020, affecting over 90 percent of youth. Continued widespread school closures during the 19/20 and 20/21 school years, left most of the world's youth learning from home. I refer to this as COVID-19 schooling, crisis schooling, or pandemic schooling. The 21/22 school year opened with in person learning and significant safety protocols. The new model of at-home learning, however, has changed education, potentially long term. More than ever in the past century, youth globally were learning from home, leaving the future of education in a crucial stage. After the dust settles from the world's unprecedented educational disruption, how will the future of schooling look? What will the future of education aim to be, what should it aspire to be, and what will the next generation of youth need? Because globally, the landscape of education is changing and in transition.

There are new approaches to education happening every day. COVID-19 has taught us and history has shown us that. Globally, we are rethinking what schooling "looks" like and how and when "learning happens." Some families that embrace DIY education today are doing so to combat COVID-19, racism, and bullying and to protect their children. With a growing infrastructure of online curricula and flexible virtual schooling options, families that once might have shied away from homeschooling are embracing it. The internet has brought online accessibility to those families that have the funds for equipment and streaming service. The library offers educational curricula and technology accessible by a current library card and available to all. The online options for home education are almost overwhelming with the amount of selection obtainable. "I believe that the integration of information technology in education will be further accelerated and that online education will eventually become an integral component of school education," says Wang Tao, vice president of Tencent Cloud and vice president of Tencent Education.[1]

There are homeschool groups for all types of alternative education methods (AEMs), with enrichment courses and social opportunities. Select states have homeschool assistance programs. Arizona, Florida, North Carolina, and Tennessee have formed education savings accounts that allow eligible parents to enhance at-home instruction with enrichment and specialized tutoring with public funding. Parents and caregivers who do not feel comfortable teaching an advanced subject can enroll youth in AP courses online. There has been a tremendous growth of "COVID-19 schooling" or "crisis homeschooling"; parents in desperation unenroll their child from disastrous schooling experiences or dramatic crisis. Many factors—COVID-19, school safety, curriculum, and so forth—can influence this act of unenrollment. Home education continues to grow, and thanks to the US Census Bureau the homeschool numbers are averaging at around 20 percent. What is inevitable is the parent will not have the school district help anymore. Where do you think these parents will turn for educational support? The strong likelihood is the public library.

When learning pivoted to remote in 2020, the US Department of Education ceased standardized testing for the 2020–2021 school year. For two decades, federal law required all students in third through eighth grade and high school to be tested in reading and math. Student scores are publicly being broken down by racial and ethnic groups and disability status. In February 2021, it was announced that testing would resume.

National Public Radio (NPR) has reported in-person learning data from Burbio. Burbio pulls content from school websites to determine whether a school is being held hybrid, full-time in-person, or all virtual. According to the Burbio website, the methodology "audits over 1,200 school districts representing 47 percent of the U.S. K–12 student enrollment in over 35,000 schools in fifty states. We use three different sample groups, which generate three different margins for error. Districts are checked every 72 hours for changes."[2] In March 2021, the US Department of Education, through the National Center for Educational Statistics (NCES), released the first in a series of schooling surveys, which has revealed that the number of students who continue to be remote due to COVID-19 is higher than Burbio thought. The survey revealed that, by early in February 2021, 44 percent of elementary students and 48 percent of middle school students in the survey remained completely remote. The survey found significant variances by race: 69 percent of Asian, 58 percent of Black, and 57 percent of Hispanic fourth graders were learning entirely remotely, while just 27 percent of White students were. During the height of COVID-19, an Illinois high school, Maine Township District 207, emailed a document called "What Is E-Learning?" to parents and caregivers. It states, "An E-Learning day is a type of learning that will occur via electronic media, typically on the internet. All students will not be required to be in the actual classroom and will check into the class via a learning management platform and complete an online assignment from the teacher." The letter went on to say to contact the school district if internet access was needed at no cost to the student. The district offers the following to parents:

Why E-Learning?

- E-Learning is better than added days at the end of the year but attendance counts!
- Move the curriculum forward.
- School is not a building; it's a collection of experiences.

Maine East High School of District 207 teaches youth "who speak 54 languages and 75.5 percent of students live in homes where English is not the primary language. The student population is 38.3 percent White, 5.0 percent Black, 20.4 percent Latinx, and 33.0 percent Asian."[3] While remote learning and virtual eLearning is working for some youth, it is not working for all. Excessive screen time, lack of differentiation of instruction, and asynchronous remote schedules have aided in the upsurge of home education led by parents. For districts with in-person learning, the concerns about overexposure and spread of COVID-19 have families opting to school from home, increasing the homeschooling rates.

EdWeek Research Center surveyed school administration across the country in October 2020, according to *Education Week*. The survey reported homeschooling in response to COVID-19 is responsible for a substantial decline in registration schools. It also reported that almost 60 percent of parents shared homeschooling as the main reason for enrollment deterioration from COVID-19.[4] While states around the country are noticing higher than past homeschooling numbers, Nebraska has seen a steep data-tracked increase. David Jespersen, a spokesperson for the Nebraska Department of Education (NDE), said in September 2020 that the state had recorded

13,426 exempt (homeschooled) students for the 2020–2021 school year, up from 8,570 in the previous year. The NDE has reported higher than average phone inquiries for exempt status, which homeschooling is called in Nebraska.[5] Nebraska is not alone; North Carolina and Wisconsin have also had a sharp increase.

The US Census has the most comprehensive data regarding homeschooling numbers and potential future implications of COVID-19. The Household Pulse Survey (HPS) is an online survey that is hosted in three phases and explores effects on education: "to support in the nation's recovery, we need to know the ways this pandemic has affected people's lives and livelihoods. Data from this survey will show the widespread effects of the coronavirus pandemic on individuals, families, and communities across the country."[6] The HPS offers a glimpse of what the future holds for COVID-19 effects on homeschooling and the future of homeschooling. HPS compares data from the spring 2019–2020 school year and the fall of 2020–2021 school year. "In households where respondents identified as Black or African American, the proportion of homeschooling increased by five times, from 3.3% (April 23-May 5) to 16.1% in the fall (Sept. 30-Oct. 12)."[7] The homeschooling numbers in 2021 are significantly higher than in previous years at the state and national levels. "Schools reflect the changes that are occurring more broadly in the society, and there seems to be no end to changes (economic, cultural, and political) that schools are expected to keep up with and even lead," according to Lorna Earl, retired associate professor from the Department of Theory and Policy Studies at the Ontario Institute for Studies in Education of the University of Toronto.[8]

Jane, a homeschooling parent from a suburb of Chicago, shared with me in March 2021, "I'm hoping that this year opens some minds about homeschooling. I would love some more resources during the day or discounts for homeschool families. Just an overall awareness is always helpful, and recognizing that it is hard work, and we don't sit around ignoring our children all day. I do child-led units, meaning I take their current interest and then find a ton of learning resources and activities to dig into the topic. I do two workbooks just to keep on track with spelling and math. My DREAM is to promote the flexibility of homeschooling. I love learning style theory and try to adjust our learning to the best way my kids learn instead of forcing them into what a system expects." She adds that COVID-19 schooling has brought diversified curriculum offerings to the homeschool market, something she felt the market was lacking before COVID-19. Jane hopes that the future of schooling and homeschooling will continue to grow in racial and ethnic backgrounds. Currently, her biracial family resides in a suburb of Chicago.

They were in Washington, DC, which she credits with being "amazingly diverse homeschool communities, with lots of military families." She greatly misses having families that reflect hers in abundance nearby.

Future of School (FOS) is a national educational society calling for and rallying US education change. The #futureofschools is the trending hashtag that works for student success, "no matter where their learning takes place."[9] "To document and forecast the evolution of K–12 education in real-time, Future of School is an organization of the people, by the people, and for the people. We work in education. We are former teachers. We are parents or have children in our lives. We advocate for a better education because a passion for learning drives us, and we care about kids. And at one time we were students, too. We are YOU," according to Future of School. The one size fits all approach to education is recognized as not being effective by the FOS. The future of schooling predicts an increase in how and when technology is used in education. Yet this transition to online virtual remote school has had quite a bit of a learning curve for students, parents, and teachers. COVID-19 has established the widespread flexibility features linked with the practice of technology in education. "Research suggests that online learning has been shown to increase retention of information, and take less time, meaning the changes coronavirus have caused might be here to stay."[10] COVID has changed education with the sudden and rapid shift to an online remote learning model—with at-home learning, which has left many wondering if this model will persevere even after the pandemic and how it will impact the future of education.

There is a shift happening in the paradigm of schooling. COVID-19 has created gaping disparities in youth achievement and intensified gaps that prevailed before COVID-19. The National Bureau of Economic Research's working paper "The Impact of COVID-19 on Student Experiences and Expectations" found that lower-income students are 55 percent more likely to postpone graduation due to COVID-19 than their more affluent peers.[11] Sadly, the study also found that the educational disruption and school closures nearly doubled the gap between low- and high-income youth. The future of schooling will need to have equity and equality of access.

The future of education centers around equity and equality of access; the future generations deserve better. As a society, we cannot point fingers at the schooling institutions or teachers for the disparities that are so blatant, currently, for many of the teachers or schools have never worked so hard learning a new way to teach. The disparities stem far deeper. The historic *Brown* Supreme Court case ended segregated schooling. Or did it? American youth continue to be schooled in racially and socioeconomically solitary communities. Illinois and New York state have the highest concentration of Black students with other Black students, 76 percent on average in both states. Black youth in these schools are isolated from White and middle-class

Figure 8.1.   Youth learning from home due to COVID-19, March 2021. Christina Giovannelli-Caputo.

Figure 8.2. Youth learning from home due to COVID-19, March 2021. Christina Giovannelli-Caputo.

students, attending schools with other non-White groups in concentrated poverty.[12] Some scholars blame the disparities on neighborhood segregation and school choice.[13] Desegregation of schools had a peak period after *Brown*; however, in recent years, it has dissipated. The universal educational system failed the marginalized youth. A separate and inadequate educational system does not produce an equitable culture or a strong democracy.

Deserting any noteworthy strategy or lawful energy to mix schools has led to cumulative seclusion of Black youth in American education. The gaps are happening state wide and country wide, which need to be addressed and fixed for future generations. A one size fits all model of education is not universal and will not meet the needs of all. Families that know about homeschooling and have access to the legalities of schooling at home are beginning to take back control of their family's education. The public library can serve and help close the gaps. Everyone has access to the public library, and perhaps our communities need to be reminded of that.

AEMs have been around for as long as education has been occurring. As children grow, they naturally learn. Learning happens all around them, and it happens differently for each child. There are brick-and-mortar schools and alternative schools that encompass the AEMs. Some homeschools encompass the AEMs too. As stated, there is no one size fits all approach to how families educate just as there is no one size fits all approach to how youth learn.

Differentiated instruction has been naturally happening throughout education and librarianship. How librarians answer reference questions is differentiated and uses different tools and aids depending on customers' needs.

How does the future of education look? There is a long history of introducing mitigations and advancements in progress for the sake of education. In 2008, interactive whiteboards (IWBs) were the "thing" of the future, the groundbreaking technology I would instill within my district with my teachers. I write this tongue-in-cheek; at the time, it was innovative. If you are not familiar, they are whiteboards mounted on a wall and linked to a computer. A projector projected content on the board that was manipulable by the student. SMART and Promethean boards led the crusade for interactive technology whiteboards. In my tenure, I introduced the ENO (another brand). An article from 2007 in *Education Week* estimated 12 percent of US classrooms had IWBs.[14] Before the IWBs, it was the DVD player, the VCR, TV, and radio. All tools are used to engage the students and progress the level of education. The Online Public Access Catalog (OPAC) automated the card catalog in librarianship, easing the customers' usability and allowing patrons to search all aspects of the library resources. The purpose of the OPAC was never to replace the librarian or library staff, merely use it as a tool to aid patrons. The same can be said for the IWBs; they were not meant to replace the teacher—they were to be used to engage the learner differently.

During COVID-19 times, youth are learning from home. The device has replaced the teacher-through learning platforms and applications. Many youths are left alone to their learning. While the intent is to replace the classroom virtually, some youths are thriving, and some are struggling. Remote and virtual schooling do not allow differentiated instruction to the level many of the students were receiving in traditional classrooms. This learning model has accelerated families to seek AEMs and schooling changes. When I was instituting the IWBs back in 2008, I thought that was the future of education. Technology has changed and advanced at a rapid pace. Never did we imagine the present state of education or the state of the world with COVID-19.

The biggest takeaway is to engage the schooling community. Listen, Learn, and Repeat. Once the library creates connections with external allies, partnerships can be made. There are ways to serve the at-home learning

Figure 8.3. Homeschooling child, Fall 2021. Christina Giovannelli-Caputo.

community, through and beyond the pandemic. Keep your pulse on the educational community, while engaging and embracing the school diversity in the area in which you serve. Programs and presence in the communities will be instrumental for igniting the community partnerships that are needed to serve fully. Often, proposals are required to institute new or expand current services, and when intentionally used, proposals can be extremely effective. Proposals are beneficial for the library and staff, but they will not build relationships needed to serve our communities. Library staff need to rethink how we serve during and after COVID-19 because relationships are necessary for community engagement. The community needs to see us in the library and out in the community. There is an inherent growing need to follow Marva

Collins and the advocates who came before. All the past advocates' footsteps have paved the way for our families' schooling freedoms in our communities. We, as librarians, should follow the example of Collins and serve through the love of the community.

It is unlikely, that centuries ago when policy makers were instilling brick-and-mortar schools as the norm and mandating compulsory attendance, they imagined the world we live in today. Schooling a century from now will probably look very different than it does currently. The remote and virtual model of learning, while not ideal for some, has bridged the gaping stereotype between home education and the traditional school.

COVID-19 has taught us that learning does not need to happen within the four walls of a classroom. Remote, virtual, or eLearning selections can expand the public school offerings beyond the traditional classroom learning environment. Technology will continue to advance and grow. Virtual, eLearning, public, private, and at-home learner schools and online platforms will expand. Families will continue to seek out AEMs that will benefit and fit with their family culture. There will be naysayers that disagree with all of the educational methods that communities and families choose to utilize. Ultimately, there is no way to precisely know what the learning community will look like in the future. However, we can predict that librarians will be deeply embedded within the community and creating partnerships that will withstand the test of time.

Thank you for the tireless work you do.

Notes

1. C. Li and F. Lanani, "The COVID-19 Pandemic Has Changed Education Forever. This Is How," April 2020, accessed March 29, 2021, https://www.weforum.org/agenda/2020/04/coronavirus-education-global-covid19-online-digital-learning/.

2. Burbio.com, "Burbio's K-12 School Opening Tracker," updated June 20, 2021, https://cai.burbio.com/school-opening-tracker/.

3. "Maine East 2020-2021 Profile," eastmaine207.org, updated January 12, 2021, https://east.maine207.org/wp-content/uploads/sites/2/2021/01/MaineEast-Profile-2020-21rv.pdf.

4. A. Prothero and C. Samuels, "Home Schooling Is Way Up with Covid-19. Will It Last?," February 25, 2021, accessed March 27, 2021, https://www.edweek.org/policy-politics/home-schooling-is-way-up-with-covid-19-will-it-last/2020/11.

5. Olivia Wiesler, "Homeschooling in Nebraska Continues to Rise," accessed March 27, 2021, https://starherald.com/news/local/education/homeschooling-in-nebraska-continues-to-rise-covid-19-could-play-a-part/article_17e8dc90-36e5-5494-ae15-3926ba2f6347.html.

6. US Census Bureau, "Household Pulse Survey: Measuring Social and Economic Impacts during the Coronavirus Pandemic," https://www.census.gov/programs-surveys/household-pulse-survey.html.

7. J. Fields and C. Eggleston, "Homeschooling on the Rise during COVID-19 Pandemic," March 22, 2021, accessed March 28, 2021, https://www.census.gov/library/stories/2021/03/homeschooling-on-the-rise-during-covid-19-pandemic.html.

8. L. M. Earl, "The Promise and the Challenge of Classroom Assessment," in Assessment as Learning: Using Classroom Assessment to Maximize Student Learning (Thousand Oaks, CA: Corwin Publisher, 2012).

9. Future of School, https://www.futureof.school/.

10. Li and Lanani, "The COVID-19 Pandemic Has Changed Education Forever."

11. E. Aucejo et al., "The Impact of Covid-19 on Student Experiences and Expectations: Evidence from a Survey," June 2020, accessed March 31, 2021, https://www.nber.org/system/files/working_papers/w27392/w27392.pdf.

12. G. Orfield and D. Jarvie, "Black Segregation Matters," December 2020, accessed April 4, 2021, https://www.civilrightsproject.ucla.edu/research/k-12-education/integration-and-diversity/black-segregation-matters-school-resegregation-and-black-educational-opportunity/BLACK-SEGREGATION-MATTERS-final-121820.pdf.

13. A. Roda et al., "Making School Integration Work in New York City Schools: A Long-Term Solution to the Enduring Problem of Segregation and Inequality," Fordham Urban Law Journal 48, no. 2 (2021): 449–73.

14. Michelle R. Davis, "Whiteboards Inc.," Education Week, September 12, 2007, https://www.edweek.org/education-industry/whiteboards-inc/2007/09.

Index

#OwnVoices, 98

1000 Hours Outside, 60
1918 Flu Pandemic, 34–35
1937 Polio Epidemic, 35
2009 H1N1 Influenza Pandemic, 35

Abington School District v. Schempp, 22
"African American Homeschooling as Racial Protection," 103
Algonquin Area Public Library, 64–65
Ali-Coleman, Khadijah, 101
American Academy of Child and Adolescent Psychiatry, 60
American Library Association (ALA), xiii–xiv, 64, 66
Arment, Ainsley, 60
Association for Library Service to Children (ALSC), xiv, 6, 63–64, 66, 82
AHML. *See* Arlington Heights Memorial Library
ALSC. *See* Association for Library Services to Children
Arlington Heights Memorial Library, xiv, 83, 87–88

Bakken, Cathy, 67
"Behind the Trend: Increases in Homeschool among African American Families," 103
Bering Strait, 6
Better Late Than Early, 21
Bishop, Rudine, 98
Better off in School, 37
Board of Education (BOE), 40
Boston Latin School (BLS), 9, 11
Bothell High School, 30
Brown v. Board of Education, 19, 100
Burbio, 108

Cathy Duffy Homeschool Reviews, 53
Carbondale Public Library, 80
Cérol, Marie-Josée, 103
Charlotte Mason, xi, 61–62
Chicago Public Schools (CPS), 102
Chiquihuite Cave, 6
child's first teacher, 5, 63
Classical Conversations, 56

120 ~ Index

classical homeschooling, 56
"Closure of Schools During an Influenza Pandemic," 32, 34
Coalition for Responsible Home Education (CRHE), 41–42
Collins, Marva, 101–102, 115–116
Columbine shootings, 31–32
common school, 6, 11–13
compulsory attendance laws, 13–15, 43
Compulsory School Attendance: The New American Crime, 14
Coronavirus. *See* COVID-19
COVID-19, xii-xv, 1–3, 26, 29-38, 44–45, 49–53, 57–58, 64–65, 67, 73, 77, 80, 86–88, 96, 103, 107–116, 121
curricula, xi, 19, 53, 58, 76, 103, 107

dame schools, 10–11
Deerfield Public Library, xiv, 82
Denevan, William, 7
deschooling, 54–55, 59
Desmarais, Idzie, 97
"Dismay and Disappointment: Parental Involvement of Latino Immigrant Parents," 99
Dumbing Us Down, The Hidden Curriculum of Compulsory Schooling, 23, 50, 101
Duyvis, Corrine, 98

early literacy, 6, 63
Eberle, Holly, 64–65
eclectic homeschooling, 53, 58
"The Education Trust," 17
Education Week, 30, 109, 114
Engel v. Vitale, 22
Escape from Childhood, 21
Every Child Read to Read (ECRR), 6, 53–64

Farenga, Pat, 21, 59
Fields-Smith, Cheryl, 100–101, 103

Florida Parent Educators Association, 99
Florida Virtual School, 44
food insecurity, 35, 37
Forrester, Amy Seto, 98
Franciscan Catholic Missionaries, 13
Free Grammar School, 9
Furness, Adrienne, xiii–xiv
Future of Schools (FOS), 111

Gaither, Milton, 22
Gatto, John Taylor, xv, 23–24, 50, 53, 101
"Get Your School Ready for Pandemic Flu," 34
Global Education Coalition, 29,
Global Home Education Exchange (GHEX), 41
Grayslake Public Library, 91
Greenleaf, Robert, 71–72
Growing Without Schooling, 20, 59

Harris, Mike, 23, 39
Harvard College, 10, 98
"Helping Your Child Succeed in School," 5
Henry, Kary, xiv, 82
Hirsh, Aaron, 95
Holt, John, xv, 20–22, 53, 59, 95
Homeschool Advisory Team (HAT), 78, 82–83
Homeschool Legal Defense Association (HSLDA), xiii, 22–23, 38–40, 42
Homeschool Resource Center (HRC), 11, 53, 89–91
Homeschool Gone Wild, 59
Honig, Alice Sterling, 5
Household Pulse Survey (HPS). *See* US Census Bureau Household Pulse Survey
How Children Fail, 20
How Children Learn, 20

I'm Unschooled. Yes, I Can Write, 97
immigrants, 13–14, 17
indigenous, 7–8
Influenza Pandemic 1918. *See* 1918 Flu Pandemic
International Center for Home Education Research (ICHER), 40
Isthmus of Panama, 6

Jennings, Cynthia, 76
Jespersen, David, 109
Jim Crow laws, 19
Johnsburg Public Library, xi, xii, 53, 89–91
Journal of Youth Services in Libraries, 77

Kings County Library System, 26
Kleist-Tesch, Jane, 77
Koch, Emily, 88
Ku Klux Klan (KKK), 17–18, 43

LGBTQIA+, 96–97
Lederman, Doug, 95
Lightfoot, Sarah Lawrence, 10
"Local Mitigation Strategies for Pandemic Influenza," 34

Maine Township District 207, 109
Mann, Horace, 11–12
Marshall, Thurgood, 100
Massachusetts Act, 9
Mazama, Ama. *See* Cérol, Marie-Josée
Meissonier, Nancy, 30
microschooling, 57
Mommy Maestra, 99
Montessori, 11, 61
Moore, Dorothy, xv, 21–22, 55, 95
Moore, Raymond, xv, 21–22, 55, 95
Moore Formula, 21–22, 55
Mount Prospect Public Library, 68–69

Nabrit, James, 100

National Black Home Educators (NBHE), 100
National Center for Educational Statistics (NCES), 1–2, 26, 49, 95, 97, 99, 108
National Geographic, 6
National Museum of the American Indian, 7
National Home Education Research Institute (NHERI), xii, 41
National Household Education Survey, 2, 95
National Public Radio (NPR), 108
National School Choice Week (NSCW), 86
Native American Indian, 7–8, 14
Nebraska Department of Education (NDE), 109
Nonpharmacological Interventions (NPIs), 32–34, 45
nature schooling, 60
Northwest Ordinance, 15

Olivera, Monica, 99
Old Deluder Satan Act, 10
Old Town Public Library, 76

Pardue, Bill, xiv, 87
part time attendance, 44–45
Parent and Family Involvement Survey (PFI), 1–2, 49, 95, 97
Penn-Nabrit, Paula, 100
People of Color (POC), 19, 97, 103
Phil Donahue Show, 20
Pierce, Walter M., 18
Pierce v. Society of Sisters 1925, 18, 43
Pikes Peak Public Library District (PPLD), 75–76
Pointer, Ann, 19
Protestant Reformation, 9, 13
Public Library Association (PLA), 6, 63

Ray, Brian, 41, 73

Reyes, Augustina, 14
Riley, Gina, 97
Robertson, Jennifer, 80
Ryan, Colleen, 91

Saint John Catholic School, 30
School Can Wait, 21
school closures, 2, 13, 29–30, 32–35, 37, 50, 107, 111
Southern Jurisdiction of Scottish Rite Masonry (Masons), 17
Sequoyah, 8
Schwartz, Robin, 80
Skokie Public Library, 80
Smith, Mike, 23, 39
Socratic method, 103
Spanish Flu. *See* 1918 Flu Pandemic
Spokane Public Library, 67
Stern, A. M., 37
Style, Emily, 98
Summer Slide, 37

Taylor, Venus, 100, 103
Tebow, Tim, 42
Temple University, 103
traditional homeschooling, 55–56
travel schooling, xv, 55, 58

Underground History of American Education, 24, 101
United Nations Educational Scientific Cultural Organization (UNESCO), 2, 29

unit studies, 55–56, 59, 61
unschooling, xi, 15, 23, 59, 62, 97, 103
US Census Bureau Household Pulse Survey, 31-32, 41, 96, 103, 108, 110
US Department of Agriculture (USDA) Food and Nutrition Division, 37–38
US Department of Education, 1, 5, 17–18, 29, 32, 38, 64, 108–109

Waldorf Method, xi, 61
Weapons of Mass Instruction: A Schoolteacher's Journey Through the Dark World of Compulsory Schooling, 23
We Need Diverse Books, 99
Weingarten, Randi, 30
Wentz, Kathy, Foreword, 53, 86–87, 91
Westside Preparatory School (WPS), 102
Whiteman-Mann, Henrietta, 7
Wild+Free, 53, 60, 61
Wilderchild, 61
Williams Institute, 96–97
Williams, Karla, 59
Williams, Meca, 103
windows and mirrors, 98
Wisconsin v. Yoder, 44

Young Adult Library Services Association (YALSA), 14, 64, 66

About the Author

Christina Giovannelli-Caputo has twenty years experience in education and librarianship. A change agent recognized for dedication and advocacy for inclusive and equitable services to diverse populations, including alternative schooling methodologies within marginalized groups. Caputo conceptualized and spearheads the "All Learners Welcome-At Home Learners and Homeschool" current initiative that has united administration, libraries and school districts to work cohesively across the nation to support diverse learners during COVID-19. She is known for increasing the professions awareness on schooling diversity, historical context of education and public libraries partnerships through; publications, presentations and professional development groups. A mom to four, she keeps busy advocating for youth everywhere.

www.ingramcontent.com/pod-product-compliance
Lightning Source LLC
Chambersburg PA
CBHW070734230426
43665CB00016B/2232